A Bridge for Troubled Souls

"I loved this book. As a survivor of a traumatic event in my thirties, I could have benefitted from this book. *A Bridge for Troubled Souls* is a step-by-step guide for Christians to heal themselves by trusting and following the guide shown in this book. These principles have already been provided to us in the Bible by Jesus. *A Bridge For Troubled Souls* is beautifully written and easy to understand. Thank you D. Franklin Bradley for this lovely book."

~ Joy A. Butler, LCSW
Trauma Therapist and owner,
The Healing Center of Asheville

"It is with great joy that I highly recommend *A Bridge for Troubled Souls*, by D. Franklin Bradley, to every person on their Christian journey who may have despondency, despair, or the emotional pain that often accompanies that journey. And also to you who have never started the journey that begins by faith, to accept Jesus as Lord and Savior which is of eternal significance. I recommend this book for two reasons: 1) It is not a theory written by D. Franklin, but it is written out of the honest experiences of his life. 2) It is based on the Word of God that will endure forever true! I can say with all honesty that if this book had been available at the beginning of my ministry, that ministry would have been more profitable and fruitful. May God bless you richly as you read and ponder *A Bridge for Troubled Souls!* "

~ Pastor Don Shockley
Retired after 69 years in ministry.

"This is a book that facilitates Bible study and one that I had next to my Bible as I read and did Bible study. This book helps to generate dialogue with God (prayer) which, to me, is the ultimate relationship builder between me and God. This is not a one-time read but a book that should be used for continuous development and encouragement throughout the Christian journey. I have an extensive library of Christian books, one that will fill an entire bedroom, but *A Bridge for Troubled Souls* is one to keep at the forefront and handy as I conduct self-evaluation and Bible study."

~ Sharvine Hill
CSI – Crime Scene Manager

A Bridge for Troubled Souls

Christian Principles to Alleviate Despair

D. Franklin Bradley

YAV PUBLICATIONS
ASHEVILLE, NORTH CAROLINA

Scripture is taken from the New King James Version (NKJV) Copyright © 1982 by Thomas Nelson, Inc. Used by permission. All rights reserved.

Quotes from Morning and Evening Daily Readings by C. H. Spurgeon used with kind permission of Christian Focus Publications, Geanies House, Fearn, Tain, Ross-shire, IV20, Scotland, United Kingdom www.christianfocus.com.

First Edition

ISBN: 978–1-937449–52–0 (softcover)

ISBN: 978–1-937449–53–7 (ebook)

ISBN: 978–1-937449–57–5 (audiobook)

Published by

YAV PUBLICATIONS
ASHEVILLE, NORTH CAROLINA

Books may be purchased in bulk for educational, business, fundraising, or sales promotional use. For information, contact info@hopesharbor.net or books@yav.com
Send correspondence to:

Gritty Liberty Inc.
PO Box 240, Bethlehem, GA 30620

Cover art and interior images by Matt Smart—Puckett Inc.

3 5 7 9 10 8 6 4 2

Published September 2021

Printed and Assembled in the United States of America

Dedicated to
The Son of God

"Come to me all you who labor and are heavy laden,

And I will give you rest.

"You shall know the truth and the truth shall set you free.

"As the Father loved me, I also have loved you…" Jesus

Acknowledgments

Most of all, I want to thank my wife Kris. She endured the agony of watching me in the crucible as God remade me.

I also would like to thank my Brothers and Sisters in the Christian faith who prayed for this project for many years. Your encouragement also helped bring me through the tough times when I wanted to quit.

CONTENTS

Preface

Have you lost hope that the future will ever get any better than it is right now? Are you feeling despair? If so, do you know principles contained in the Bible can relieve the despair you feel? I can tell you it's true. I survived depression by applying them.

I wrote this book to share the discovery of God's love for all people, especially those in despair. You know, that sickening dread convincing you things will never change? And because of despair, depression is likely present also. Knowing God loves us should bring hope. But feeling trapped in despair and depression makes it difficult to even hope things will improve. It's the quintessential vicious circle.

Despair is a mindset, a belief producing feelings associated with hopelessness. Such feelings are real, even if the reasons for it are not. Despite those feelings, there is hope for you, and you can change no matter how bad things are right now. The difficulty is finding what gives hope, and that's where this book comes in.

Victor Frankl wrote that to survive despair we need a reason to live for the future, a hope things will work out alright. I believe he meant a change of perspective leading to a changed mindset.

Ridding yourself of despair starts in your mind by changing how you think about and perceive circumstances causing problems.

If you don't trust the Bible already, let me assure you, please. I've tested and tried principles from the Bible and discovered by trial and error it is worthy of your trust. I use applicable principles to help manage PTSD (Post-Traumatic Stress Disorder) arising from violence during childhood and from 21 years in law enforcement.

This book does not focus on depression, or PTSD, or even despair, per se. Instead, its focus is implementing Biblical principles.

This book is not intended to replace professional help. When depression becomes ingrained, professional medical intervention is necessary to manage it. If you are currently under a doctor's care for depression, ask the doctor before reading this book. If you do read this book, I hope you create and strengthen your spiritual life by applying what you learn here. And as good as that is, it doesn't have to end with these Biblical principles.

God not only desires to heal your soul but also wants a loving relationship with you.

Jeremiah 29:11 contains this promise, "For I know the thoughts that I think toward you, says the LORD, thoughts of peace and not of evil, to give you a future and a hope."

God's value of you is where your true identity resides. God created you in His image. Think of this: the Son of God died for you so He could forgive you. What more can He do to prove His love?

Dare to believe God wants to heal you.

Dare to do the work involved in the process.

Apply the Biblical principles to come.

D. Franklin Bradley

May 7, 2021

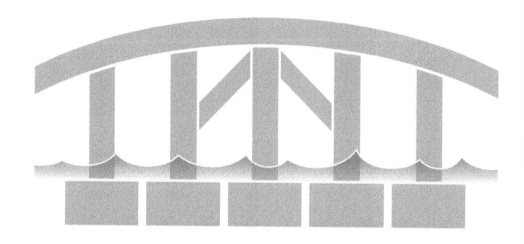

Introduction

The bridge image shows how using spiritual principles instills structure into your life. The images provide a visual sense of progress in the work of restoring hope. When given time to develop, feelings of hope will reduce despair.

Remember: the key to success is not to focus on getting rid of despair or depression. If you do, it will only deepen them.

Instead, focus on the progress made during each chapter. Allow the truth to work its power. This process eventually alleviates despair fueling depression. Then give it time.

If drawn out, it would look something like this:

Focusing on positive thoughts = flushing out despairing and depressing thoughts.

If you change your focus, it changes your mindset. Despair decreases as a result of different thinking habits as they develop with time and practice.

Now, changing the mindset or outlook, this is everything. It helps if you have a tool to bring about change. That tool is Biblical principles. Consistent applications are the method of use. When used, these principles often lead to a positive difference in life. The results are inevitable.

A positive change in thinking causes the chains of despair to fall away.

The Son of God promised in John 8:32, "And you shall know the truth, and the truth shall make you free."

Now, about the bridge theme. It came to me while flying home from South Asia. I woke from a deep sleep and the image of a bridge came to my sleep-fogged mind along with a verse from Luke 4:18. I sketched on an envelope as the idea developed. I had no idea what this verse had to do with anything, but was sure God gave me the basis for a book.

Later, while looking at the drawing, I wondered how to develop the theme further. Then, I remembered George Patterson's teachings about the Seven Commands of Christ.

With foundations in place, the Seven Commands could be the uprights, or structure. I added this to my illustration. Okay, Jesus laid the foundations with what He promised in Luke 4:18. And now a Christian puts spiritual structure in place. To do this, we follow the teachings, commands, and exhortations of Christ. This analogy worked, but then what?

A bridge without a span on top to walk on is useless. What if the span represented the Fruit of the Spirit listed in Galatians 5:22, 23? I read verse 25 of Galatians 5 where Paul urged Christians to walk in the Spirit. This worked. I completed the drawing using each aspect of the Spirit's fruit as planks.

I had the image now, with the conceptual form for the book itself laid out in three parts. Part One contains the promises of Jesus as foundations. Part Two, the basic commands of Jesus as the structure. Part Three, the Fruit of Jesus's Spirit as the span or bridge deck.

A reminder before going further. Any knowledge learned is useless against despair until put to action. Yes, some information is useful without actually practicing it. But in this case, the knowledge is comparable to the difference between knowledge of a cure for cancer and applying the cure. All medicines for the body work this way to heal and psychological healing of the mind is the same.

Applying *A Bridge for Troubled Souls* is progressive work. This is intentional. It's meant to help you see the principles, when applied, put spiritual structure into place. This enables you to change and rise above mental and emotional tormenting despair. Do you see how the bridge image gives a type of metaphorical structure? One you may stand on as standing on certain truths or principles. This is how to rise above and cross over, to come up out of trouble and put it behind you.

Let me give a bit of encouragement here about how this is an ongoing process. It may be hard to think about the work involved in this, but if you won't give up, something good happens. Replacing despair with a positive mindset helps motivate you to keep going.

This is necessary to prevent you from slipping back into darkness again. Listen, I fear depression. As soon as I start slipping into it, I check my focus, make corrections, and get back on the solid deck of the bridge. You can do the same.

This book isn't meant to be a rigid formula to follow, but a guide along the way. Be patient with yourself. It likely took a while to get wherever you are. The same goes for finding life without despair. If you do the work, you will feel better as you go.

If you want to work and apply lessons contained in this book you'll need a Bible. Before going further it may help to reiterate issues contributing to despair.

Despair is sometimes the typical result of abnormal circumstances, abuse, or trauma. If you're depressed, it does not mean you're crazy, no matter what it feels like. Examine these sources of despair as examples only, and see if you recognize any:

- Abuse during childhood—physical, sexual, mental, emotional
- Mental trauma resulting from assault or the presence of violence
- Abuse from a spouse, whether physical or verbal
- Abandoned by a caretaker or spouse
- Constant strife in relationships
- Not enough resources to make ends meet for extended periods (utter poverty)
- A problem child in your home
- A problem or wayward spouse
- Mental or physical disabilities
- Combat—it inflicts many military personnel with PTSD so complex I can't begin to go into it. Despair is a hallmark of PTSD, revealed by the abnormal rate of suicide among combat veterans.

Additionally, public safety personnel also have more than their share of despairing circumstances and exposure to violence. (They are also subject to PTSD and ever-increasing hopelessness in a society becoming indifferent to their sacrifices.)

The preceding list of causes for despair is not all-inclusive. This is because we shouldn't focus on the depths of despair, there's no point in doing so; no crucial point to unearth. Instead, the focus must be on how to relieve it. I can't express enough the importance of being careful where you allow your mind's attention to roam.

Consider this verse if you want to guard your mind: Philippians 4:7, "and the peace of God, which surpasses all understanding, will guard your hearts and minds through Christ Jesus."

PTSD

A brief word about PTSD—The key to understanding the cause is in the acronym.

Post-Traumatic Stress Disorder. Trauma is the villain here.

Violent assault, especially sexual assault, is horribly traumatic. A mental health worker once told me the trauma of sexual assault is the cause of so much PTSD among youth. It's also a leading cause of self-mutilation and eating disorders.

The Three Steps of
A Bridge for Troubled Souls

☞ One—The foundational promises Jesus made early in His ministry
☞ Two—The basic commands He gave during His ministry when obeyed and used bring the hopes of Step One to life
☞ Three—The results of following the commands are seen in the way a Christian lives. These results are evidence of change taking place.

In Step One, we study the foundations for a change in life. Jesus established foundations. He made five promises in Luke 4:18, and these are quoted in full in Chapter 5 of this book. Jesus did the hard work already. He put foundations in place that are unlike those of the Leaning Tower of Pisa. Have you seen that thing lately? It looks like any moment it's going down.

Not so the foundational promises of Jesus. His reliable promises are important enough to examine in depth. By this we gain understanding of their authority and learn how to release the inherent power.

The five promises: Salvation—Healing—Deliverance—Sight—and Liberty.

A note about releasing power from Jesus's promises: the Word of God contains authority for Christians to live by. This is like the code of law by which law enforcement officers conduct their duties.

Belief in the promises is similar. Studying the Bible gives the foundation of authority granted to every Christian. Faith, as duty, acts on that knowledge to build change.

Step Two is the action and application required to change your life. The seven basic commands of Christ provide the structure. Each command is like a girder welded to the others. The first two commands are one-time events. Repentance (unto salvation, although repentance unto sanctification is lifelong. More about this later) and Baptism. The five remaining commands are implemented daily. Those five commands are: Communion—Love God and Others—Prayer—Give—Teach (Make disciples).

Apply these to the best of your ability, daily. No perfection required.

Step Three is where the results, Fruit of the Spirit, become evident. The fruit comes from living out the Seven Commands. Galatians 5:22 & 23 list the Fruit of the Spirit which is analogous to good works. They are Love—Joy—Peace—Patience—Kindness—Goodness—Faithfulness—Gentleness—and Self-control. These are aspects of good character. When viewed like planks placed on top of the bridge structure, they form the span. This is the deck of the bridge upon which you walk throughout life. They are also like markers along the way to measure change. We'll go through each of these in-depth.

Step One

Laying the Foundation:
The Word of God

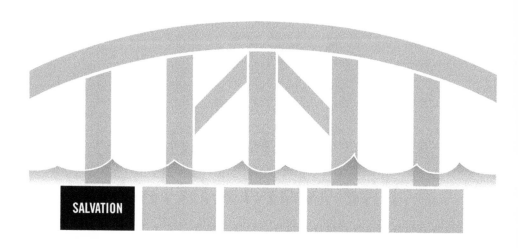

SALVATION

CHAPTER 1

Salvation

**"He has anointed Me To preach the gospel to the poor;"
Luke 4:18**

**"For God so loved the world that He gave his only begotten
Son, that whoever believes in Him should not perish but
have everlasting life." John 3:16**

"You must be born again." John 3:7[1]

I N LUKE 4:18 JESUS CAME TO preach the gospel to the poor.
The word gospel means good news, glad tidings. What good
news did Jesus bring? Forgiveness is available from God to every
person who chooses to receive it.

For a blessing, Christian, look at all you have in Christ:

   ☞ His righteousness—As He is in God's sight, so are you.
   ☞ His perfection—God sees you perfect in your spirit.
   ☞ You remain accepted in the Beloved.
   ☞ You are one with Christ as His spiritual body or bride.
   ☞ You have His guarantee you will go to Heaven, for His Spirit
      seals you.

I know Christians believe the truths listed above. Yet, we must
understand all Jesus accomplished on that cross. Otherwise, we
live like spiritual paupers even though our Father in Heaven owns
the treasury.

We have these blessings because of what He did on the cross. Look at all that happened as a result of Jesus's death:

- ☞ Atonement—The price paid for sin's penalty satisfied God's wrath.
- ☞ Redemption—With sin atoned for, God redeemed us from slavery in sin.
- ☞ Regeneration—God began a work in our spirit to open our hearts.
- ☞ New birth—Upon asking God's forgiveness, we have new life.
- ☞ Justification—We inherited eternal life.
- ☞ Sanctification—The Holy Spirit works continuously to perfect us.

It is important to review the good news Jesus proclaimed and also review the results of His death. After any review of the cross, the primary detail to ponder is the atonement that provided the means for God to forgive sin. Atonement is the key that unlocks all God's other gifts covered later in this book.

After being saved, many Christians stop thinking in-depth about their salvation. They may go to church and strive to fulfill their idea of the Christian life. However, they may find something missing; there is emptiness in their heart. Instead of peace and joy, guilt often haunts the child of God.

If children of God are wholly forgiven, from where do feelings of guilt now come? Have you had such feelings since becoming a Christian? What was your explanation for those feelings? Have you dealt with them to the point that they are no longer present? Or is there still a floating dread that somehow something's not quite right between you and God?

Such questions are common. You can find the answers to these questions through a fresh examination of salvation.

When Jesus accepted God's punishment for sin, it was a one-time act of atonement. He took our place of punishment. This alone makes it possible, upon repentance, to become God's forgiven child. No more guilt is necessary. Forever.

What about the Christian who sins after salvation? We've all done it. According to Paul in Romans 3:23, "all have sinned, and come short of the glory of God." The legal basis for the pardon provides the answer and points to the wonder of Jesus's sacrifice. When Jesus stood condemned in our place, His act of doing so cleared the way for us to approach God. It also justified God to move further on our behalf by adopting us. He does this on a legal basis because we are no longer under the spiritual death penalty. A Christian's relationship with God is now one of Father and child. I reiterate this due to how easy it is to miss out living in this reality: Almighty God is our Father.

The new spiritual life you hold as a Christian came from a new birth. It's why Paul wrote in Romans 6:4 "...just as Christ was raised from the dead by the glory of the Father, even so, we also should walk in newness of life."

This new spiritual life is but a gateway to other good things; one of which is eternal life. And life here demands a response from you. It may be that those demands have you on the ropes. But there is a purpose for you to fulfill in this new spiritual life. One that intends you to fulfill your destiny. And that destiny is not found by wallowing around in guilt.

There are two kinds of guilt at issue here. The first is guilt for sinning against God before you were a Christian. It is the guilt removed by accepting God's forgiveness. For you now stand innocent. The second kind of guilt forms when a Christian sins and the Holy Spirit convicts that Christian's heart. This should bring that person to repentance, to turn away from any particular sin.

This is an important distinction. When you sin as a Christian, there is no divine wrath attached to that sin. When you confess known sin and repent, meaning you turn from that sin, it restores you to innocence, though there may be lasting consequences of your sin. (Second Samuel, Chapter 10–12:10 recounts the dire consequences of King David's sin with Bathsheba.) After you repent, any feelings of guilt are false-guilt. Satan uses this false-guilt to keep Christians trapped, locked in spiritual bondage. Faith is the key to this lock, the belief you remain forgiven.

Salvation is thus the crucial foundation to our faith. Without salvation we cannot build a relationship with God. When the need for salvation goes unresolved, it is like building a bridge on sand.[2] The correct foundation must be in place first. This is what Jesus did by giving us the only approved means: His atonement for sin.

[For anyone not a Christian please allow me to explain. Sin can be resolved in one way only. Every person must accept the atonement Jesus provided when He died on the cross. Forgiveness is yours if you want it. You must ask God for forgiveness, and show your sincerity by turning from all known sin.]

Recognizing the rock-solid value of a good foundation based on the total forgiveness of God is crucial. This recognition helps you live above circumstances of trouble and pain. In Romans 8:1 Paul writes, 'There is therefore now no condemnation to those who are in Christ Jesus, who do not walk according to the flesh, but according to the Spirit.' Paul wrote 'therefore' because, in the previous chapter, he lamented his own battle with sin.

Therefore, Christian, there is no condemnation of you no matter what you've done. But some will ask, "Are you saying there are no consequences for sinning?" I didn't say there are no consequences, rather no condemnation.

Consequences for a Christian choosing to sin is like putting your hand into boiling water. The damage depends on the duration of immersion, as immersed in willful sin. You can get burned by sin, but God doesn't condemn you. He will lovingly discipline every erring child (count on it) to protect them from the harm associated with sin.

Get a grasp on this truth, though. You are never condemned as a Christian no matter what consequences you're in right now. Healing in the heart begins with confessing sin to God. Forgiveness follows repentance and leads to obedience to God's Word. This places a spiritual foundation in your life.

Actions to Consider

On 3x5 cards write one or more of the following and put them where you'll see them throughout the day:

- ☞ There is no condemnation because I am in Christ Jesus. (Romans 8:1)
- ☞ I did not receive the spirit of bondage to fear, but I received the Spirit of adoption, so I now say Abba Father. (Romans 8:15)
- ☞ The Spirit bears witness with my spirit. I am a child of God and as His child, I am an heir of God and joint-heir with Jesus. (Romans 8:16 & 17)
- ☞ I know that all things work together for my good because I love God, and He called me according to His purpose for me. (Romans 8:28)

Once you've done this, you now stand on the first foundation of your faith.

Final Thought for this Chapter

Jesus came to set us free from the self-condemnation of a broken heart. And He promised to heal the brokenhearted.

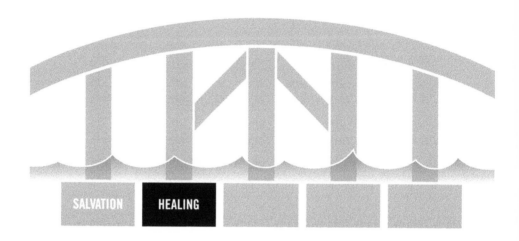

CHAPTER 2

Healing

"He has sent Me to heal the brokenhearted." Luke 4:18

"He heals the brokenhearted and binds up their wounds." Psalm 147:3

DESPAIR AND A BROKEN HEART OFTEN go together. Is it logical Jesus intends to heal broken hearts by relieving despair? Yes.

The word brokenhearted in the Hebrew and the Greek means shattered in pieces. The heart in Biblical terms refers to the mind, will, and emotions. To heal brokenhearted people means God restores wholeness to mind and spirit. He bandages spiritual wounds to make His children feel secure in the way they think and feel.

If you need healing for your heart what will it take?

It's normal to look out at circumstances and think if certain things changed it would help heal a broken heart. Changing living conditions may be part of the process, but not always. That process starts within your mind by changing the way you think. I say this because God at times leaves circumstances as they are. This teaches several lessons, each one adapted to a person's needs. (Even then abusive relationships are not God's will.)

Otherwise, when Jesus allows suffering to overtake a person it is to impart a spiritual lesson. The way physical pain motivates a person to seek a doctor, emotional pain should motivate us to seek God. If you find God in your sorrow, ask Him to teach whatever lessons He wants you to learn before He heals you. I know this is tough to do. Listen to me: it's better to learn God's lessons now than to come back for remedial training later.

While in the 3rd year of marital separation, I lived with a buddy and worked evening watch. My routine when ironing a uniform included music. Once when I was ironing, Agnus Dei by Michael W. Smith started playing. Sadness and emotional pain surged through my chest. As that song played, I knelt and begged God to take away the pain.

In that moment, I knew God planned to teach me something by allowing my anguish to continue. Since I didn't relish having to come back for remedial training about the lesson, I asked God to leave me in the circumstances, leave me until I had learned every lesson he would teach me by way of the pain and suffering. It may not make sense, but I wanted the pain to mean something, I wanted to gain from it.

God is merciful, so He didn't leave me in pain any longer than necessary. With time, He allowed me to heal and move on.

The lessons learned? The most important lesson was how necessary for the health of one's soul is living close to God and experiencing how much He loves us. Talking about God's love is not the same as experiencing it.

For me, the experience of living in God's love occurred only after reading John 15:9 first thing every morning and last thing every night for 18 months. This practice carried me through the tough days. Even now, it continues to keep me mentally strong enough to live in joy most days.

When healing is applied to emotional pain, it involves release or resolution. Our hearts can hold a great amount of pain, and, when in deep distress, it's natural to seek a way out, to find a release from the pain. This is not surprising. Pain by its very nature demands release. However, seeking relief from pain is where many get into trouble with addictions. If you don't find a healthy release or escape soon enough, your heart goes searching for relief wherever it can find it.

Be warned. Unresolved pain accounts for several mental and emotional disorders, including acute anxiety, OCD, and unrealistic fear, etc. Unrelieved pain may also lead to deep anger. It's understandable, even inevitable, that some deep-seated rage can develop from chronic pain. You may have heard the saying "Anger is like acid; it eats away the container holding it."

Are you in unbearable pain right now? Do you want to know why? Do you wonder what possible good can come out of it?

To answer your question, consider this: One purpose of pain induced by depression is to make us pray. Eminent theologian Charles Spurgeon called trouble the "hounds of hell" that chase us to God for relief. When a child of God seeks Him during heartbreak, they find He is a God of comfort and compassion.

Another good aspect coming from pain is when you connect with God on a deeper level. Only emotional agony brings about deep intimacy with God if you so choose. Yet another purpose for this deep level of anguish is that it creates empathy. Only those kind souls who have experienced profound hurt can empathize with us. Someday, you may understand a hurting soul who crosses your path, and, by your understanding, you will bring comfort to this wounded soul. Doing this for others will redeem some of your suffering by giving purpose to your loss.

No matter the depth of pain, don't let it go to waste. Some of the most significant people in history attained their noteworthiness through painful circumstances. They received the lessons pain had imparted and used them for the good of others.

It's time to revisit Romans 8:28. "And we know that all things work together for good to them that love God, to them who are the called according to his purpose." Consider what circumstances might be excluded from the promise that all things work together for good? Do you think "all things" include the pain of betrayal, divorce, wayward child, death of a loved one, sexual abuse, physical abuse, addictions, and the loss of all held dear as the result of those addictions? You can add to this list no doubt. However, no matter how much you add, the promise covers all things. Good comes to the ones who trust God to bring good out of the bad things in life.

*[By the way, if I missed listing what you're going through, take
a moment to write it down, and then write Roman 8:28 under
it. Keep this handy and read it often while God is working. After
He heals your heart, burn that piece of paper.]*

It may help to pause here and consider a wonderful attribute of
God's nature. The Bible contains the fact God is love.[3] It doesn't say
God has love, though He does. It doesn't say God will love—though
He will for all eternity—it says God is love; it's the very core of His
nature.

About Blame

Even if the pain is your fault, God still loves you. He allows the suffering to last not one second longer than it takes to impart the lesson. For
one thing, it teaches us the seriousness of consequences for sin. Even
then, when God disciplines, He does it in love. It's the same way any
good father takes a firm stand against willful wrongdoing in a beloved
child, such as a two-year-old playing in the street. By this, I mean His
corporal punishment is nonetheless loving, and it is administered only
to protect His loved one from further dangerous behavior.

God is a good father.[4] His faithfulness ensures the healing of
your broken heart.

Actions to Consider

☞ Write down a few thoughts and feelings you have about
the pain you are experiencing right now. Write it in a
column on the left side of the page. Write the cause(s) of
your heart's deep hurt. Put in that column whatever comes
to mind while thinking about and feeling the pain. It
doesn't have to be neat or pretty. And it's okay to include
any anger or rage. God already knows what you're feeling.
He won't be surprised.

☞ Opposite your list, on the right side of the page, put Bible
promises addressing each item of suffering. If you are new
to finding such information in God's Word, Christian book

stores, including those online, offer booklets of God's promises in the Bible. These are usually categorized by topic and
you may find God's promises useful encouragement related
to what you wrote in the left column.

☞ Keep the list handy, and refer to it from time to time while
going through later chapters. Doing this exercise allows a
displacement to occur. Healing thoughts based on God's
promises flush out destructive self-defeating thoughts. The
latter are what destroys your heart and mind. God's promises
also serve as medicine for healing your mind and mending
your wounded heart.

Healing is the eventual release from pain and despair. In the spiritual realm, healing requires perseverance. You must stick it out. The
challenges are, first, submitting to spiritual surgery. And second,
allowing the healing process to take as long as it requires. The book
of James reveals the purpose of trials is to test your faith. This testing
develops perseverance. Perseverance must finish its work: that of
imparting maturity to the believer.[5]

Spiritual maturity is necessary. This means you must strengthen
your faith through Bible reading. A strong faith helps to bring you
out of the past and into a place of healing. Healing begins the process
leading to the next foundation—Deliverance.

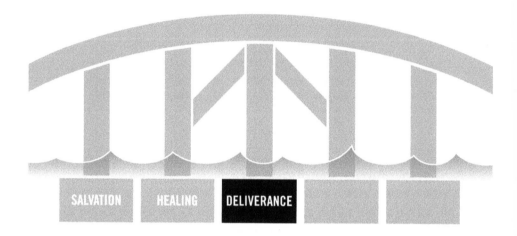

CHAPTER 3

Deliverance

"O wretched man that I am! Who will deliver me from this body of death?" Romans 7:24

Jesus said He came, "To proclaim liberty [deliverance] to the captives." Luke 4:18

I N THE BRIDGE IMAGE FOR THIS chapter, the foundation of Deliverance is midway. It supports the structure's central pier. On the cover you see dark water under the bridge. This depicts trouble. Deliverance is the crucial foundation rising out of deep, dark troubles. It represents the work of God to free His children from destructive habits. And free them before they arrive at a prison camp of bondage.

First Samuel Chapters 29 and 30 is an account of David and his followers' families. Raiders captured the women and children while David and his men were away. When the men returned to their base in Ziklag, they found it burned to the ground. Raiding Amalekites had taken their wives, children, servants and livestock. The effect of the raid caused David and his men to weep until they had no strength left. Then, David's men talked of stoning him. They blamed David for the loss.

David asked God in prayer what he should do. God instructed him to overtake the Amalekites and recover all without loss. And so David followed God's instructions and delivered the captives. It is the same with us and the promise of Luke 4:18 stated at the beginning of this chapter.

The word that Jesus used for deliverance also means freedom or liberty. Here, it implies being brought back from captivity before it's too late to change direction, before bondage deepens. In the case of lost souls, God rescues them from the road to hell. In the case of Christians, God delivers them from destructive habits leading to more pain. This foundation enables us to rise out of smothering confusion before it sweeps us away.

Although Jesus already made provision for deliverance, the process defies logic. Case in point: Years ago, when separated from my wife, I once told a pastor I could not stand another minute of the pain. He dared sit there and tell me it could take months, even years, before I was free. In anger I told him, "You have no idea what this is like! I don't need you to give me some Christian cliché."

He sat calmly observing me over folded hands held under his chin, compassion in his eyes as he studied me. He pointed to a picture of a young woman on a credenza behind him and said his experience with an event in the life of his daughter, about which he provided the details, had given him an understanding of deep pain. During that time, he once thought his heart would burst.

In the silence that followed, I realized this pastor was trying to prepare me for the days ahead. In kindness, he told me what I needed to hear. Still, it was a bitter pill.

The pastor was right; it took more time than I had expected before the process of deliverance ran its course. But I have to confess, by the end of the process, which lasted several years, I had been healed.

Also, I discovered a positive aspect to the process as I muddled through those days: God began my deliverance by degrees according to how much I could handle. He never kept me in the fiery crucible a second longer than necessary. In the end, I realized that fear and dread of the process had been worse than the experience, itself.

The fear subsided with time as I began to understand the reasons why I suffered so much in that mess. With eventual clarity, I knew the consequences were from events covering many years of my past. A picture formed in my mind as I sifted through past mistakes. I saw where they formed a pattern. And most of this occurred in the years since I became a Christian. I saw I had to make changes now to avoid the same mistakes in the future. I needed to break the habitual patterns and ensure my deliverance remained a way of life. The first pattern I had to change was from a negative mindset to a positive one.

Another benefit of the process of deliverance by degrees was that it slowly provided hope as I progressed day by day. Despair lessened some, and confidence gave spiritual quests traction. I began to see where past sins had led me to bad habits, captivity of behavior. Some of the habits were my attempt to numb-out by, for example, viewing pornography, which releases dopamine, a heroin-like substance in the brain. Similarly, I sought respite in the oblivion produced by consuming excessive alcohol. These pain-driven habits led me into a destructive lifestyle.

Your pain may also drive you to find relief in destructive ways, meanwhile neglecting to protect yourself. The desire for comfort is especially true when depressed. Once you reach a particular point of despair, you may no longer care about the consequences. You find a way to rationalize your methods to numb the pain, and this rationalization is dangerous ground. When you arrive at this point, spiritual sight and insight are necessary to not only see the facts and danger of it all but to see some hope in your future. Without perceiving a basis to hope that things will get better, who would ever change for the better?

And so Jesus gave Sight as the next foundational promise.

Before turning to the next chapter, this is an excellent place to ask: Do you have any harmful, destructive practices or behaviors and habits? This book is about change and this point is the perfect place to begin. I offer the best encouragement I know: be courageous, face the changes needed right now. To quote another, "If not now, when?"

Actions to Consider

⚠ Are you dabbling in addictive behaviors? Take stern action now to stop before an addiction gets its hooks in you. Look at the following list. Do you see anything you feel you can't or won't live without? If so, please find a resource to help you become free before it's too late.

⚠ Porn: Filter programs are available for electronics. These will protect you.

⚠ Alcohol: Many programs exist to help become free of this chemical.

⚠ Other drugs regardless of whether prescribed or illegal. Sometimes drug use requires medical intervention for withdrawals. See a doctor if in doubt.

⚠ Gambling. This includes lottery tickets—enough said.

⚠ Eating disorders.

If what you're struggling with isn't listed, write it down. Then, do all it takes to become free.

If you're not sure about what to change, much less how, then the following chapter on Sight is helpful. Ask God for the help offered by His Spirit. Then read the next chapter paying careful attention. Ask God to remove any veil from your mind, and then wait for insights to come to you by reading God's Word. The book of Luke is a good choice to read alongside the next chapter.

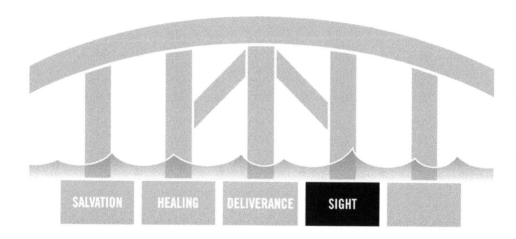

CHAPTER 4

Sight

"And recovery of sight to the blind," Luke 4:18

**"One thing I know: that though I was blind, now I see."
John 9:25**

*[There is an account in the Bible, the whole of John Chapter 9,
when Jesus healed a blind man. It's a great story and worth the
time to read now, if possible.]*

IT IS A FOUNDATIONAL NECESSITY TO see and understand
spiritual issues related to your life. Without this spiritual vision
no one understands the Bible as God intends. Therefore, the
Spirit of God must take away any veil over your mind. Subsequently,
God's Word may be studied and analyzed. Many have done so
and claim expertise. Still, I'm not talking about lifeless intellectual
knowledge of Biblical facts. While intellectual knowledge of God's
Word is formidable, even essential, you need more than this in the
struggle against despair.[6]

A few years ago, I walked the beach on the final morning of my
vacation. God spoke to my spirit, asking me if I wanted the veil
removed from my mind. I knew what veil He meant. I was blind to
pride and arrogance. And I tended to compartmentalize events in
my life and not deal with certain problems, like anger. After thinking
about what the process might entail, I said, "Yes."

Since God hates pride, He took issue with mine before allowing
me to complete this book. The same with anger. God has many ways

to humble a man or woman, and He used several of these on me. Now, my first reaction, not my initial thought, is normally compassion and patience instead of anger and loss of temper, I'm better at doing a slow burn. I'm no poster child for a humble, peaceful man, but the effect of reducing pride and anger are evident, and I now have more peaceful moments. This encourages me to prayerfully ask for more of having the "eyes of my understanding opened," as Paul prayed in Ephesians 1:18.

Sometimes, even with the best of intentions our understanding remains dark. Christian growth involves learning to come into the light, as God is in the light. When we do, we learn how much more there is to learn. Learning the principles of God is a lifelong event. It comes and goes in intensity with experience. At times, learning comes easy. The Bible becomes a fountain, and Jesus bids us drink. At other times we read and immediately forget what it said. It is normal to forget and demonstrates why learning and spiritual enlightenment are daily needs, like eating. Some of us can go several days without food and not notice much effect other than a sense of hunger. But, if a week goes by without food, the human body becomes feeble. Is not spiritual life the same?

To see the importance of spiritual nourishment, think of it this way: It's like working out with weights. There is a positive result when you take in enough protein and carbs and then hit the weights. You can hit the weights longer and harder after the right nourishment. Spiritual disciplines are no different.

Believing in what you cannot see but for the eyes of faith depends on spiritual sight. This same spiritual sight is required not only to understand and learn the Bible's teachings but also to apply what you learn. Finding God's will is seeing how to implement Biblical knowledge to ascertain what choices in life are best.

In the early eighties, I wanted to know from God whether or not I should move to Colorado. Being a new Christian put me at a disadvantage when I prayed for the purpose of determining God's will in the matter. I prayed the best I could, but didn't know how to hear God's voice. I tried to read the Bible for guidance, but couldn't understand what I was reading. One evening I went up on a nearby mountaintop and beseeched God for help. Nothing happened.

So, I took it on myself to move out there anyway and let the consequences arise, come what may. The move was a disaster. After several weeks, I returned home with $11 to my name. It took years to recover financially. So what caused me to make such a mistake? I was an immature Christian, true. And I prayed, but as far as I could tell, God was silent about my pleas. Why hadn't I seen that the correct decision was to stay where I was?

My problem leading to this disaster was spiritual blindness. A lack of understanding, like a veil, kept me in the dark. This prevented me from making a better decision when the desire to move first came about. The spiritual sight I needed at that time developed only later by reading God's Word, studying it as you would an operations manual. I hadn't done this in the years before the need to know God's will. I was not a student of God's Word partly because I refused to attend any church, but church attendance was only part of what I needed. I also required excellent Biblical teaching by men like Chuck Swindoll, James Dobson, J. Vernon McGee, and Charles Stanley. Unfortunately, I didn't discover the teachings of these men until a couple of years after the move.

I could've sought Godly counsel from a wise Christian. Well, remember that pride thing? In those days, there was no way I would allow someone to tell me what to do, as in tell me not to move to Colorado. Though I couldn't see it at the time and despite my best efforts to stay there, God intervened and brought me back to Georgia that same year.

The first time knowing God intervened in my life occurred one day not long after praying. While driving to work, I listened to the radio. Chuck Swindoll was teaching a series called Living on the Ragged Edge. He said something that shocked me; he confided that he was no longer surprised at the number of suicides in our country. Rather, he was amazed there weren't more, even mass suicides, given what he was reading about despair in the book of Ecclesiastes. (His insights helped me when I descended into suicidal depression two years later.)

I had never heard of Ecclesiastes before this and also never listened to a preacher talking like he did. Besides, he was on the radio where anyone could listen to him! Couldn't he get in trouble? I mean, he was much too honest in my ignorant opinion. Regardless, the preaching hooked me.

I began reading the Bible as a result and read it with insatiable hunger. I read it in the morning before leaving for work, during every break, and during lunch. I couldn't get enough. More than thirty years have passed, and I still remember the joy of those days. The joy from understanding what I read. So, what brought about this change, to cause this hunger for God? Looking back it was simple. My spiritual sight had opened.[7]

After those days, spiritual sight helped when anxiety and stress became overwhelming. It happened after a tough shift at the police department where I worked. I came home and lay across the bed, my head hurting so bad with a headache that tears ran down my face. My wife told me I needed help, professional counseling. Even though I didn't want to talk to anyone about my problems, especially someone I didn't know, I agreed. Because of the pain, I had to find relief.

Listen to me, please. You may be hesitant about going to counseling, but you need to know there is nothing wrong with seeking help. It doesn't make you weak. Many survive trauma from their past, in part, due to the effectiveness of counseling. It is worth the effort and the costs involved. Please believe it is okay to find the help you need.

Actions to Consider

☞ Take an online assessment to see how you score concerning issues such as chronic depression, anxiety, fear, and PTSD if you've experienced trauma.

☞ See your doctor for further assessments, if necessary, and for a referral to professional counseling.

☞ Continue to pray for understanding, to see how best to proceed with a change in your life. When the blind man in John 9 called out to Jesus, He asked what he wanted done for him. The man said, "Lord, I want to see." Your prayers asking to see won't be the first for Jesus. He's waiting to hear from you.

The final foundational promise Jesus gave in Luke 4:18 has to do with freedom from spiritual prison. It's being released from a dungeon of the soul. This promise is vital when trying to break free from the bondage of addictions. Anyone tangled in the web of pain-numbing practices, take heart.

Spiritual vision is a portal to spiritual liberty.

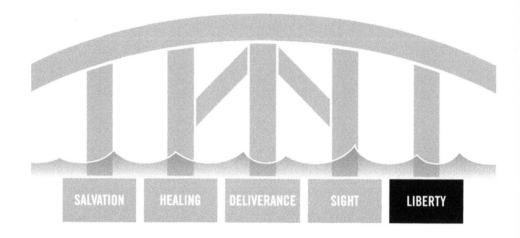

CHAPTER 5

Liberty

"To set at liberty those who are oppressed." Luke 4:18

"without shedding of blood there is no remission [liberty that comes when sin is forgiven]." Hebrews 9:22

In the Band of Brothers miniseries, an army patrol comes upon a prison camp. The soldiers are appalled at what they see. Even after enduring several months of combat and bearing the brunt of Nazi brutality, they are unprepared for the gruesome effects captivity had on those prisoners within the barbed-wire compound. Emaciated men stumble to the fence. Bodies of the dead lie scattered about the camp. A runner returns with the commanding officer, Major Winters. He orders the gate chain cut and his soldiers enter the compound. A half-dead man staggers up to a soldier and embraces him, weeping.

This stark scene portrays liberty for prisoners. Spiritual deliverance is just as real though not so evident. It takes faith to see the reality of freedom. The Son of God gave the promise of deliverance and a life free from sin's condemnation. It is one of the foundations of a life free of despair.[8] Salvation is part of our deliverance. But again the blessing doesn't have to end there. Other things in life also demand deliverance; addictions, for instance.

This final foundational promise is complex because of everything affected by it. When I did a word study for *liberty*, I discovered the word rendered in Greek is not only the same word used for deliverance, it is also the same word for remission used extensively in the New Testament. It describes the work done by the cross in providing forgiveness (remission) of sin for all who desire it.

Luke 4:18	Isaiah 61:1
"The Spirit of the Lord is upon Me,	"The Spirit of the Lord God is upon Me,
Because He has anointed Me	Because the Lord has anointed Me
To preach the gospel to the poor;	To preach good tidings to the poor;
He has sent Me [a]to heal the broken-hearted,	He has sent Me to [a]heal the broken-hearted,
To proclaim liberty to the captives	To proclaim liberty to the captives,
And recovery of sight to the blind,	And the opening of the prison to those who are bound;"
To set at liberty those who are oppressed;"	

The promise of liberty is a result of Jesus in action. It looks like this when Luke 4:18 is listed as an action guide:

1. Jesus was sent to preach the gospel, the good news of forgiveness.
2. He came to heal the brokenhearted, hearts broken by sin and its pain.
3. He proclaimed deliverance available to captives.
4. Jesus made the restoration of sight for the spiritually blind possible.
5. He remains present to set free those oppressed by sin.

Isaiah 61:1 is the corresponding verse to Luke 4:18. In Isaiah, liberty is the same as opening a prison or dungeon for those bound by sin. Here addictions clutch people with a grip of iron, chained in bondage.

When Jesus declared His commission in Luke 4:18, He first used the word liberty for those who, like a prisoner of war, are marched off to prison. However, this fifth promise is for those who already arrived at the concentration camp of addictions and mental disorders—buried in bondage, trapped behind bars of iron. Listen, if this is you, Jesus knows what you're going through. He knows how it feels when you have no hope.

Please don't be offended by the term mental disorders. I have PTSD, treatment-resistant depression, and anxiety. They are disorders, the result of exposure to violent trauma. In my case, the violence was long-term; for others, one-time events can similarly wound the mind. There is nothing to be ashamed of if you carry scars from abuse.

Because of my experience with the bondage of porn, PTSD, and depression, I've longed to write this chapter on liberty. I admit feeling a little daunted because there is a power at work opposing liberty. This power has its roots in the different causes of bondage. In my own experience with addiction and mental afflictions, the power is pain-driven and rooted in the deep part of my survival instinct.

[A side note about the force within us resisting efforts to overcome addictions, depression, anxiety, and the host of others disorders:] I mentioned how the power is rooted in my survival instinct, and by this I mean in the mid-brain. There is a subconscious effort going on to ensure survival. When something threatens us with danger, this part of the brain reacts to cope with the menace. If we cannot deal with the danger, the feeling, subconscious or not, is that we will die. At this point, the survival instinct kicks in.

When a child is too young to understand the presence of violence, this primal instinct to survive looks for a way to cope, to find comfort to ease the feelings of distress. The mind finds relief from stress by releasing chemicals in the brain. These are dopamine (a heroin-like pleasure hormone) and serotonin (a mood elevator), both of which are neurotransmitters. The feelings of comfort from these substances become equated with coping, as in "I feel good, so I am coping." Do you see the hook in this?

The ultimate outcome occurs when someone learns how to release these chemicals through the use of multiple outside stimuli (porn, drinking, drugs, eating, gambling, cutting, etc.); a dependency develops over time. One comes to believe that the presence of stimuli equates to life, while the absence of stimuli equates with death.

I discovered the survival instinct remained strong even though at times I wanted to die. It isn't logical, but remember, we're not talking about logic, per se. The survival drive goes beyond logic because these chemicals affect the primal parts of our brain.

During all the counseling and programs I attended, I never heard mention of this phenomena until recently. However, understanding the part played by the survival instinct revealed why depression and anxiety may become treatment-resistant. Recently, I began a process of renewing my mind in keeping with Romans 12:2. I had to choose to believe the truth, the truth that I'm not in danger of perishing. So far, my body craves the feelings that come with the dopamine dump and the battle lines are clear. What remains is whether I choose the dump or freedom from depression and anxiety. Logically, the answer is freedom. But, physically, even mentally, I crave the dump. I have to believe that with enough time, I will replace the physical and mental demand for comfort by refusing to provide for the dopamine. At the same time, I will work on lessening the depression and anxiety with the truths of Scripture. For example: by reading Ephesians 1:6 "to the praise of the glory of His grace, by which He made us accepted in the Beloved."]

Romans 12:2

And do not be conformed to this world, but be transformed by the renewing of your mind, that you may prove what is that good and acceptable and perfect will of God.

Another daunting fact is freedom doesn't come overnight. This is tough for those who are in a prison of your mind, though there are exceptions. The hard truth is everyone who determines to be free must make a choice sooner or later—the choice to take responsibility for past decisions and current actions.

On a positive note, I found when ridding myself of porn, there are a couple of quick and easy ways to move things along. The primary one at the time was disconnecting the Internet from my home. It immediately kept me from viewing porn on my home computer, a victory in itself. The other long-term fix I used was installing a porn-blocking filter.

If you can cut off contact with the sources of things pulling at you and calling your name, then do it! There's no middle ground here. Half efforts = full failure.

Yet another power resisting freedom is denial.

Denial is a significant hurdle in 12-step programs and detox regimens. It is the dividing point between those who want to be free and those who refuse to believe they need to be free. It can be hard to persuade an addicted person to admit they have a problem in the first place. Such denial is a powerful tactic for the mind to avoid facing mental pain. With so much pain at stake, it is a difficult habit to overcome. If this is you, meet the pain, admit you're addicted, get help and let the truth work its power over you.

To be free you first must decide to take positive steps toward freedom. This decision will likely involve getting help from family and friends. When possible, consider pastoral support. Many pastors are trained to recognize situations that require professional counseling. They may also provide references to programs like Celebrate Recovery.

Actions to Consider

☞ If addiction is even a remote possibility, take an online assessment. These help give an idea of where you may be on the addictions' scale.

☞ If you want treatment, you may find that your insurance plan covers the treatment of addictions.

☞ Pastoral counseling (if you know a trusted pastor or minister). Don't go in with blind trust. Your trust of any counselor or pastor is crucial to success.

☞ Finally, be honest with yourself. Having an addiction doesn't make you a bad person even if providing for that habit led you to unlawful behavior. Repent, decide to fight the thing holding you prisoner, and enlist the help of others.

After the introduction to Step Two we'll begin the next chapter, Repentance. The decision to become free is a type of repentance when it necessitates changing course. Repentance breaks the bonds of denial. Repentance enables you to change the course of your spiritual path.

Two important thoughts have underpinned this chapter, and you should carry those over to the next section.

1. Jesus promised liberty. By His divine authority and power, it is yours to appropriate, if you truly want it.
2. You who want this freedom must first see the need for it, and then ask for freedom, in prayer. By faith (faith is a choice to believe despite your feelings), accept the process as God leads you into a new life.

The next section takes a look at the Seven Basic Commands of Christ. These are principles God requires every Christian apply. If you do, it enables you to become sound in mind and spirit. If you're ready, you have a part to play.

Step Two

Raising the Bridge Supports: The Seven Commands of Christ

Raising the Bridge Supports:
The Seven Commands of Christ

"Blessed are those who hear the word of God and keep it!"
Jesus in Luke 11:28

THIS SECTION IS ABOUT BUILDING THE bridge structure upon the foundations. It's an excellent place to look at different aspects of bridge construction.

What makes for proper bridge construction? It involves rock-solid foundations, sound structure, heavy-duty spans, and decking. Additionally, regular maintenance is necessary. To help with applying the next step, a few examples of how not to build a bridge, spiritual or otherwise, are helpful.

What will collapse a bridge? Several factors and forces will do it and in the past have brought bridges down.

In 1940, the Tacoma Washington Bridge, subjected to high crosswinds, began to sway. The span hanging suspended from cables increased motion until the center part collapsed. This event, caught on film, is dramatic to watch. The cause of the bridge collapse was faulty engineering. A result of cost-cutting measures. Our God, in His Word, gave the design for a sturdy bridge, one to withstand the storms of life. And He never cuts corners.

On December 15, 1967, a defect in only one supporting link on the Silver Bridge at Point Pleasant, West Virginia, caused it to collapse. The bridge fell when loads heavier than designed for, along with poor maintenance over a period of time, brought the structure down.

Not to worry. On your bridge ,God's structural commands have no defects. Spiritual structure withstands the load of obedience placed upon it. This Biblical structure is made up of daily obedience to His building principles. These are set forth in the blueprint instructions, the Bible.

In April 5, 1987, heavy flooding washed away a pier foundation to the Schoharie Creek Thruway Bridge in New York. The resulting collapse of a portion spanning that flood-swollen stream was eventually attributed to insufficient protection of the foundation against scouring, which is the washing away effect of moving water. A lack of proper inspections allowed the undermined foundation to go undetected. This caused it to sink and bring the affected span down; it might as well have been built on sand. On the other hand, the foundations put into place by Jesus are anchored to the bedrock of God's mighty power. And that unshakable bedrock undergirds a life-bridge built on the teachings of Jesus instead of sand.[9] Floods of opposition come against the life-bridge of every Christian. Demonic opposition scours away at the foundations not established on Bible truth. But the Biblical foundations in Christ are sure, they never fail.

Final example: On May 2, 2002, a river-barge veered out of control when the pilot blacked out. The barge struck a pier to the I-40 Bridge in Webbers Falls, Oklahoma, and brought down a section of it. In our lives come negative impacts brought on by events and people. However, every aspect of God's structure erected by applying His commands and teachings withstand those onslaughts from others. Even the ones that leave us at times feeling more dead than alive.

God is the master engineer. His blueprints for building structure into a life always work out for good. To follow God's design ensures success. This part of the book is laid out somewhat in logical order for the ease of study. Yet, your experiences may differ from others living the Christian life and that's okay.

Let's look at the first command to repent. This concerns being saved—salvation—a one-time event for the non-Christian. But, repentance leading to a Christian's sanctification is the one studied here. Sanctification means set apart. Set apart for God and set apart from the practices of the world around us. Sanctification is a lifelong process as well as the responsibility of the Holy Spirit to bring it about in every willing Christian. And it holds true for every obedient Christian.

Besides salvation, there is another one-time event: baptism. According to the Bible, this command requires a person to be baptized only once.[10]

The remaining five commands are an ongoing experience.

While going through this next section, remember: obeying the commands of Christ forms the very superstructure of a life of freedom. Obedience to Jesus's teachings brings the intended result of this study: to reduce despair. Right actions give purpose to life, a necessary component to hope. Also, remember: hope lessens pain and depression and may remove them altogether.

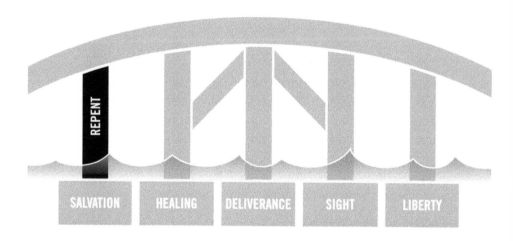

CHAPTER 6

Repent

"As many as I love, I rebuke and chasten. Therefore be zealous and repent." Jesus in Revelation 3:19

A BRIEF REVIEW IS USEFUL HERE. That's because repent has two different connotations in Scripture. The first, covered in Chapter One, is a necessary component of salvation. The connotation is not to earn salvation, but willing to turn from death to life. That kind of repentance is for non-Christians. In other words, becoming a Christian involves a willingness to turn away from a life of sin and turn to a life of obedient holiness—not perfection, but striving for it. Is anyone who is not willing to repent from committing willful sin truly a Christian? Jesus said we determine by the fruit (actions as evidence) the kind of tree, whether good or bad (whether a person is living in repentance or willful sin).

The following verse explains the need for this type of repentance.

"Repent, therefore and be converted, that your sins may be blotted out, so that times of refreshing may come from the presence of the Lord, and that He may send Jesus Christ, who was preached to you before, whom Heaven must receive until the times of restoration of all things." Acts 3:19–21a.

The second type of repentance for Christians is the focus of this chapter, that of turning from all known sin. This type of repentance should be a daily process. It is necessary to keep the relationship with God open. Repentance is also the training ground for Christians conducted by the Holy Spirit.

To repent as Christ commands in Revelation 3:19 involves feelings of regret. This leads us to turn away from sinful behavior. This level of regret causes us to think differently about the sinful behavior in which we indulge. Having a repentant heart is a gift from God. Repentance leads to love, joy, peace, patience, kindness, goodness, faithfulness, gentleness, self-control—the "fruit of the spirit" described by the Apostle Paul in Galatians 5:22–23. These characteristics are evidence a person lives for God, even though at times we all fall short. Regardless, when the fruit is missing we are still God's children, deeply loved.

> *[A note here about people who are not Christians: they may exhibit love, joy, and peace, etc. Many people imitate attributes of the Christian life to some degree. But real evidence is supernatural and doesn't flee in hard times, not even in the face of death. For examples of this, read* Fox's Book of Christian Martyrs.[11]*]*

How does someone live for God, especially in the post-Christian era of the Western world? Does it require living separated from the world, hiding from worldly influences? There are some people who believe this. Monks and nuns, for example, make a sincere effort to obey God and live for Him, but God's Word also explains in detail that separating oneself from worldly ways is not accomplished by being "taken out of the world."[12]

In John 17, Jesus prayed for His disciples, as well as for those of us destined to become Christians later. He asked God to leave them, and by implication to leave us, in the world and keep us from the evil one. Jesus asked this so we may remain free from the destructive practices of the world's systems. He then said we are not of the world just as He is not of this world.

By the phrase "not of this world," Jesus meant He was not a part of the world's belief system. The belief system of the world, especially today, involves practices and principles centered on selfish living. The ultimate result of living for selfish reasons is seen in crimes against others. In some countries we see the selfish actions of dictators and repressive regimes. Human history validates this viewpoint. Antithetical examples are individuals and nations whose efforts are for the welfare and protection of the weak. They live in the world, but, for the most part, do not put themselves first. Though I know there are exceptions.

Still, what does this have to do with repentance? Only this, it's turning away from the world's system of living for one's self. Instead, you live for God and others, by His prescribed wisdom, and according to His order. Then what does repentance look like in everyday experience?

One example is a person who habitually finds fault with people they dislike. This behavior usually comes out of a superior mindset. This worldly mindset must be forsaken to keep our relationship with God thriving. You see, God must resist the proud person because pride fuels feelings of superiority.

God frees us from this worldly mindset of superiority when we repent. But this is only one example of the intrusive influences of the world upon us. Repentance helps us recognize that the faults we see in others are present in us, too. How could it be otherwise since we're all cut from the same spiritual cloth?

Repentance allowed me to see the truth about myself as a fault-finder and to uncover where those tendencies are rooted (in low self-esteem). Now, when I see a fault in someone else, I see them as a Brother or Sister. Repentance, when applied like this, is the gift from God mentioned earlier. Only God can allow me to see something lacking in myself enough to change the behavior. And when it happens, it is spiritual sight working for me.

One last thing about repentance before going to Baptism in the next chapter: God does not mean to beat us down about our faults. He just wants us to see the need for confession and repentance because confession and repentance are the crucial means of becoming free from harmful mindsets, arrogance and pride. These negative mindsets can and will disturb our relationship with God to the point of despair and also impede our growth as Christians. The process of repentance allows us to become free of self and to love and feel empathy for others.

Actions to Consider

If you could change one thing about yourself right now, what would it be? Is it a sinful habit or depressing circumstances?

☞ For sinful behavior, confession and repentance is a must. If time permits, write the sin and beside it your confession. Putting it in writing makes it real.

☞ When not viewed in light of God's control, depression invariably leads to self-pity. Pay attention to this: Because self-pity will slide you into the bottomless pit of despair, I urge you to resist feeling sorry for yourself. Fight back by remembering good things about yourself whenever self-pity raises its hideous head.

Repentance is turning away from harmful thinking and habits and then turning to the ways of Jesus.

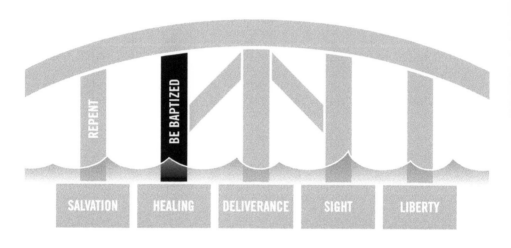

CHAPTER 7

Be Baptized

"He who believes and is baptized will be saved, but he who does not believe will be condemned." Jesus in Mark 16:16

A T FIRST GLANCE MARK 16:16 SEEMS to require belief *and* baptism before someone may be saved and become a Christian. The second part of the verse refutes this implication by stating those who don't believe are condemned, and Baptism is not a determining factor.

Baptism is an act of obedience for all Christians to fulfill. It's the result of becoming a Christian, not the cause. It's an analogy for being buried with Christ and raised to walk in newness of life.[13] Other than the ritual of submersion, baptism alludes to changing our mindset, symbolizing the renewal of our minds.

> *I was baptized in a swimming pool, and when I came up from under the water, I looked and saw the moon overhead. That's what I remember. Why mention it? Because nothing else happened. I expected some spiritual experience to occur, not the heavens opened, but at least something I could feel other than climbing out wet. So, my first feeling as a Baptized-Christian was disappointment. It was because my expectations at the time were skewed.*

Before John baptized Jesus he objected and said Jesus should baptize him instead. Jesus told John the reason He came for baptism was to fulfill all righteousness. By this, He meant since John's baptism was a sign of renouncing sin, Jesus would continue the ritual of baptism as an outward sign of an inward work. Jesus didn't need this for Himself although He always denounced sin. He gave us an example to follow and the Apostles expound upon this ritual in later writings, especially the writings of Paul.[14] When John baptized Jesus in the Jordan River, the heavens opened and the Holy Spirit came down and rested on the Son of God.[15] The same is true for us, though we don't see it.

Baptism for the Christian is an act of one-time obedience. It is not salvation. If being submerged in water could rid me of the guilt of sin then why did the Son of God have to die a horrible death? In Ephesians 2:8, Paul wrote we are saved by grace, not by works. Baptism then is an act, a work of obedience, sometimes referred to as an ordinance or sacrament.

It is necessary to look at the false teachings surrounding baptism from the spiritual viewpoint. Human pride wants to add an act or ritual of human effort to show human worth. This is done in spite of the Word of God, which states in Romans 3:12, "there are none who does good, no not one."

It harkens to the fact that if there were a way to receive God's forgiveness for sin other than the Son of God dying on that Roman cross, Jesus would have been the first to acknowledge it. When He struggled in prayer the night before His arrest, Jesus knelt beneath the olive trees in a garden called Gethsemane and asked God for another way to atone for sin.

Jesus agonized in prayer to such an extent blood seeped from His face. He asked God, if possible, to remove the coming crucifixion. He knew God was not only going to pour out the holy wrath against the sins of the human race on Him, but at that point, God would turn away from His beloved Son, unable to look at sin residing on Jesus, not in, but on.

As Jesus hung on the cross, He died and thereby completed receiving the punishment for sin.

Now, consider the fact that Jesus asked God the Father if there were any other way to punish sin other than His death. No other way was provided. This reveals to us the only way to Heaven is through death on Jesus's part—faith on ours.

Follow this sensibly—baptism doesn't avail anything here, how could it? Some who teach otherwise cite Acts 2:38, "Repent and be baptized every one of you in the name of Jesus of Nazareth for the remission of sins, and you will receive the gift of the Holy Spirit."

There are two points to bring out about this verse in Acts. First is the context. Peter said that to men who asked what they should do in response to a sermon he gave on Biblical history. In Acts 2:14–37, Peter told them to repent and by this he meant repent unto salvation. He then goes on to say they should "be baptized in the name of Jesus of Nazareth for the remission of sins."

The second point in this passage is the word "for," as in "for the remission of sins." It's the Greek word *eis* which means "to or into." The phrase means having reached or entered a purpose such as baptism, a visible act resulting from an unseen spiritual birth.[16] You could paraphrase it "be baptized in the name of Jesus because of the forgiveness of sins." Furthermore, Scripture must be interpreted in light of other Scriptures on any given topic to prevent the cultic practice of taking a verse out of context and then building a system of religion upon a single misused verse. Therefore, other Scriptures declare salvation is received as an act of faith, not through the ritual of baptism.

Baptism points back to what Jesus said the night He instituted Communion. Matthew 26:28, "This is my blood of the new covenant, which is shed for many, for the remission of sins." Remission here means forgiveness.

Actions to Consider

☞ If you've never been baptized, consider it as a loving act of obedience. When considering a pastor for baptism, steer clear of all who tell you baptism is all that is necessary for eternal life. The pastor who baptizes according to the Bible will ensure you have settled the issue of salvation before being baptized.

☞ If baptized after becoming a Christian and subsequently joining a church, beware if they tell you only that specific church's baptism is valid. It is a cultic practice. Find some other church. (In fairness to Godly pastors and their staff, it is justifiable if they inquire about your conversion experience and whether you have been baptized since becoming a Christian. I recently went through such a process when joining a new church.)

The next chapter is a turning point of sorts. We leave the nuts-and-bolts of the last few chapters and enter into relational aspects of Christianity, starting with Communion.

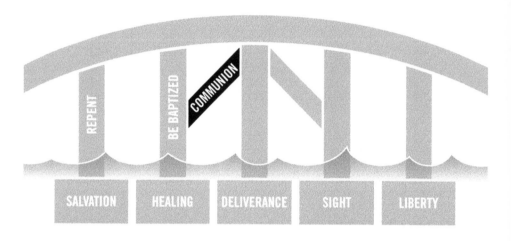

CHAPTER 8

Communion

"And He took bread, gave thanks and broke it, and gave it to them, saying, 'This is My body which is given for you; do this in remembrance of me.' Likewise, He also took the cup after supper, saying, 'This cup is the new covenant in My blood, which is shed for you.'" Luke 22:19, 20

AN ODD OCCURRENCE HAPPENED THE NIGHT Jesus was arrested. His enemies were closing in and breached the ranks of His closest followers. They bribed one of them.[17] Money replaced loyalty for a few coins of silver. The amount they paid the traitor was the going price of a slave. The betrayer divulged the location where Jesus sought refuge later that evening, shelter from the recent confrontations in the city. There the soldiers could arrest Jesus without a large crowd interfering.

But before his arrest, Jesus spent the brief time He had left with His beloved disciples. They found a place, an upper room, in which He and His followers took their last meal together. This was the Passover meal. God had instituted it after rescuing the Israelites from Egyptian slavery.

The name Passover came from the act of a death angel as it swept through Egypt one night. The angel struck dead the firstborn of every man and beast. Well, not every man and beast. The angel passed over the dwellings that had the prescribed blood of a spotless lamb, one without blemish, painted on the outside doorframe. God had instructed the Jews to take a branch of hyssop, dip it in the blood, and paint the blood around the frame. Hyssop is an Old Testament symbol of cleansing through transferring the blood of sacrifice to the sinner, and a New Testament symbol of faith, in effect putting their faith in the blood of the sacrifice. This event also involved a meal to commemorate the occasion before the angel came in the night.

The symbolism to Jesus as the Passover Lamb is evident. John the baptizer described Him as the Lamb of God. The book of Revelation describes Jesus as the Lamb slain from the foundation of the world[18] because His blood shed unto death satisfied the wrath of God.

The Passover meal helped God's people remember how He saved them from Egyptian slavery. Jesus likewise wants to be remembered as the Savior who gave his blood to save us from sin-slavery. While celebrating this final meal, Jesus continued to teach. He knew His time was short and poured out His heart to those with Him in that upper room.[19] He wanted them to remember certain aspects of His life so that they stayed close to Him spiritually. It was during that last supper Jesus gave the rite of communion as a way to remember His imminent act of love by dying for them, and us.

During the meal Jesus broke a piece of bread and handed it around to his twelve disciples. He told them it represented His body and they all received a piece of bread. In John 13:26, John watched as Jesus dipped a piece of bread into a soup or gravy and handed it to Judas. Judas took and ate it, and then he left the gathering. Now this is important to note: Judas partook of the bread, but never drank from the cup representing the blood. You see, the body of Jesus was broken for all in that He died for all people. Judas partook of Jesus's heavenly gift as tasting it, then turned away from faith; Hebrews 6:4–6 describes this principle: Judas having turned away could not be restored to repentance, because to do so would be crucifying the Son of God all over again. Only faith in the blood has saving power for those who apply it to themselves. Judas likely departed without salvation because he didn't partake of the blood of Christ, represented by the cup of wine. Did he repent unto salvation before hanging himself later on? I don't know. Scripture is silent on the matter.

What is known is that Judas left a traitor and went to his doom soon after.[20]

With the traitor gone, Jesus passed around a cup for all to drink and explained that it represented His blood.

John also described in detail how Jesus opened His heart. Five chapters in the book of John, Chapters 13–17, are devoted to what Jesus taught and shared that night.[21] These chapters contain comfort and promises as well as instructions. Matthew, Mark, and Luke recorded additional lessons Jesus taught, including prophecies for the end times,[22] but John's account is more relational in scope. While the synoptic gospels of Matthew, Mark, and Luke describe events as they occur, John's gospel reflects upon events well after they took place and with the depth of meaning that is only possible from such a perspective.

Going back a bit, Jesus began His final Passover in this life by washing the disciples' feet. He wanted them to remember: serve one another. To help prepare them for His crucifixion, He said He was going away and gave them this command: love one another. Jesus comforted His followers with the reminder: trust God. He told Thomas that He is God and therefore knew their faith would be tested.

Jesus then shifted His teaching to an analogy of how a human being can relate directly to God and stay close to Him. He tells them this parable: He is the true Vine, His Father is the vinedresser and His followers are like branches of the vine. They cannot bear fruit or create good works in and of themselves any more than a branch by itself, separated from the vine, could bear fruit. He told them the life of a believer abiding in obedience to His teachings would show evidence of that obedience. The evidence is good works that will withstand the fire of God's judgment at the at end of time.[23]

Furthermore, He wanted them to remember how their lives were connected to Him, joined to Him for all eternity. And by this truth they will never be alone. He reminded them to live in the world with confidence even if the world and its systems hate them because of the gospel message. He commissioned them to bear witness to all they've seen and heard Him teach. They must remember His words to gain strength, for, as only Jesus knew at that time, in the coming years, most of them would be put to death for their beliefs.

Jesus then prayed for Himself about His pending death. He prayed not only for the followers there with Him but also prayed for all who would come to believe in Him through their message (that's you and me, Christian).

Around the table sat rough men, some fishermen, one a zealot, another a Canaanite (outsider to the Jewish faith). What did they think as Jesus prepared them for His coming death? The Bible says they couldn't understand it, their minds were blinded.[24]

It would require the coming of the Holy Spirit before full understanding came.

After Jesus rose from the dead and appeared to many of His followers, He gave final instructions to the eleven disciples before ascending into Heaven as they watched.[25] In the Book of Acts, this same group banded together and prayed with one accord. As Jesus instructed them, they waited in Jerusalem, anticipating the baptism of the Holy Spirit. (Don't confuse this with water baptism; it's different.)

God's Spirit arrived ten days after Jesus ascended to Heaven. It was during a festival called Pentecost, the Greek name for fifty. Named as such because Pentecost comes fifty days after Passover. At this point Peter assumed his leadership position once more. He was teaching on the day of Pentecost and the group heard a sound from Heaven. It filled the house. The writer of Acts described it as a rushing mighty wind.[26] The Holy Spirit came as promised.

I once stood briefly in a mighty rushing wind. It was on a thin rock ridge in Arches National Park, near Dark Angel. When a blast of wind hit, I had to lay flat on the rock to keep from being blown off. My son Jared was there with me. He started laughing, you know, that laugh when something is ridiculous. I laughed with him as the wind beat us without mercy. Even now the memory of that wind is vivid.

Jesus wanted His followers to remember the day His Spirit came in mighty power. He left us with a written account so we can recognize it too. As for experiencing the Holy Spirit's presence, mine has been more an influence on my thinking, not a physical awareness.

Actions to Consider

☞ The next time you take communion read through John Chapters 13–17. Be sure to confess any known sin before taking the symbolic body and blood of Christ.

☞ You can take communion at home on occasion. Try bread without yeast. Bread without yeast isn't necessary, but it is a reminder to avoid the spreading effects of sin symbolized by leaven. I use pomegranate juice because it's bittersweet. Bitter reminds me of the agony of Jesus's death and sweet the eternal life to one day enjoy.

Only by the Spirit dwelling in a Christian is the new life more than merely following rituals. The new life is not reduced to keeping a set of rules, trying to please God and earn His favor. Living by rules and rituals while not grounded in love is legalism. This was the deadly sin of the Pharisees, the group of religious people who put Jesus to death. They did so after He repeatedly confronted them about the legalistic bondage they imposed on God's people.

Opposing legalism is God's love. Jesus wants this remembered first of all. We know this because Jesus declared to love God and others is the greatest commandment.

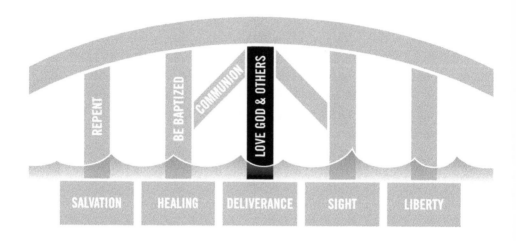

CHAPTER 9
Love God and Others

"God is love." 1 John 4:8

BEFORE LOOKING AT THE COMMAND TO love God and others, there's something every one of us should know, and I mean know by experience. God loves *you!* Knowing intellectually God loves you is different from knowing it in your heart. I speak first to the heart.

Christian, if you doubt God's love for you, then know God loves you with love so deep it is immeasurable. He hovers over you with affection. His thoughts toward you are loving joy, longing for the day you believe this in your heart. John 3:16 says for God so loved the world He gave His only begotten Son so that we who believe will have eternal life—eternal life lived with God, in His presence. No matter how you may feel about yourself or about where you fit into God's plan, Jesus will present you faultless before the throne.[27] You are the workmanship of the Son of God. He uses your failures for eventual good.[28] Any pain you're in, God understands it all. Jesus by experience knows what you're going through, and He hurts for you.

You see, even when a child of God willfully sins, God still loves that child. He will discipline every child belonging to Him, but not in wrath. God's poured out His entire wrath on Jesus as He hung on that cross. If you still have trouble believing you're loved, consider:

> When God completed creation and viewed the work
> of His hands, He saw it was good. God was pleased
> with all He brought forth, and this means the crown

of creation: people. God had spoken of these people before bringing humans into being, "Let Us make man in Our image ..." Genesis 1:26

Now, since God created us in His image, and when He viewed us as a people and saw His creation was good, how are you excluded? Be careful answering this question. It's one thing to regret past mistakes, but quite another to reject God's love for you even in the pain of such mistakes. Satan lies to every child of God, and especially when he can use your past against you to convince you to doubt God's love.

God loved us even when we were His enemy. Romans 5:8, 10 says, "But God demonstrates His own love toward us, in that while we were still sinners, Christ died for us." And "For if when we were enemies we were reconciled to God through the death of His Son, much more, having been reconciled, we shall be saved by His life." The phrase "saved by His life," means protected by Jesus. We are told in Colossians 3:3, "For you died, and your life is hidden with Christ in God." See that? Your life is hidden with the Son of God's own life and protected in God.

Dear Brothers and Sisters, if you still doubt God loves you consider: divine love allows God's love to be for you, personally. It is a love that surpasses any guilt you feel or any failure on your part. His love negates all condemnation against you. Read through Romans 8:1 right now. Do it slowly and ask God to open your heart to the great blessing of confidence in Him. It helps to pray Ephesians 1:17, 18.[29] Dare to believe this promise is yours. Now, before you exclude yourself, yet again, ponder one last effort to convince you of God's love.

When Jesus was dying on the cross, a group of priests were there taunting Him. It wasn't enough that Jesus was suffering a torturous and excruciating death by their treachery. They mocked Him with a challenge by saying if He were the Son of God, then He should come down off the cross. If He did, they said they would believe Him. Good thing for them and us Jesus did not take the easy way out.

Instead, He prayed, "Father, forgive them, for they do not know what they do."

Jesus did not exclude those men from the love of God, and you aren't excluded either. That's the emotional aspect of God's love. Now the duty.

We must learn to love God, and love others, therefore the following command:

"You shall love the LORD your God with all your heart, with all your soul, with all your strength, and with all your mind; and your neighbor as yourself." Luke 10:27

In this "Parable of the Good Samaritan" (Luke 10:25–37), a lawyer asked Jesus how to inherit eternal life. Jesus asked him what the law of God had to say about it, and his understanding of it.

The lawyer quoted Luke 10:27. Jesus commended him for his answer. You see, to love God is the way to eternal life and to love God is to obey Him and He said to believe in His Son. By this, God meant believe in His atonement for sin, not to earn it by loving God. That would be works-based salvation. Loving God is a circular process of sorts. A loving relationship with God ensures the Christian resists willful sin. The avoidance of sin enhances the bond of love for God and leads to loving others. When we love others we are in essence loving God.

Jesus said in Mark 12:29, this command to love God is the foremost commandment. And the second is like it; love your neighbor as yourself. By this declaration, Jesus equated loving God and others as integral to a well-rounded life.

What is it to love God? Paul wrote in Ephesians 3:18–19 that he prayed his readers would understand, or comprehend, the love of Christ that surpasses knowledge. This passage reveals there must be an understanding of how much God loves us. To understand the deep love God has for each one of us will lead us to love Him the more. The question is: how can a human being experience something divine, something the Apostle Paul said was impossible to know in the intellectual, scientific sense? I believe he meant knowledge leads to involvement.

Think of the mutual love experienced between two people. This kind of love gives and also gets in return. But, you must take care here, don't give love to get love. If you try that with people for whom you have no affinity, you're in for disappointment most times. When you give thoughtful considerations for difficult people, do it for the Lord's sake.

Scan through the four Gospels and read accounts where Jesus encountered hurting people. You'll experience a beautiful truth. Jesus always met every need and granted every request. He even wept with those who lost a beloved brother and later wept over Jerusalem. All because He loved each person He encountered, and loved the city, full of all kinds of people. The results were Jesus's followers loved Him in return.

Mary Magdalene loved Jesus to the point she stayed by Him at the cross and then followed the men who buried Him to see where they laid His body to rest. Early on the morning of the third day she was first at the tomb to anoint His body.

Another Mary, Mary of Bethany, sister of Martha and Lazarus, loved Jesus to the point she sat at His feet when He visited their home, instead of helping her sister serve their guests. Mary went so far to anoint Jesus with an expensive ointment one evening, an extraordinary display of her love and affection.

Another woman, who remains unnamed, also anointed Jesus all the while weeping as she kissed His feet, and wiped them with her hair. The disciples condemned the act, but Jesus defended her love for Him. He rebuked his host for not showing common courtesy to Him. But Jesus commended the woman, even though described as sinful. He said because she loved much she was forgiven much.

And then there is Paul. After Jesus changed his life, the man could not keep from expressing his love for Jesus. If you'll take the time to read Romans through to 2 Timothy in one sitting, Paul's love for Christ is evident, clear, and solid.

The irrefutable fact is Jesus loved with words and deeds every person who came to Him in sincerity. His compassion for suffering people overflowed to them. Consider this: what made them any different from you and me? Did Jesus love them more because they were of the Jewish race? No. God doesn't show favoritism. Though the Pharisees thought He did.

They believed God excluded them from obedience to the spirit of the Law. They were masters of following the letter of God's law, but this only led to pride and hypocrisy, wickedness which Jesus vehemently condemned. That same pride and hypocrisy also contributed to the downfall of the Jewish nation when they rebelled against Roman rule. To put down this rebellion, Roman general Titus destroyed Jerusalem in 70 AD and sent the surviving Jews to the four corners of the Roman Empire.

It's without a doubt a hard command to follow, to love others. It's tough because Jesus included the command to love our enemies and do good to even those who spitefully use us.[30]

Let's go back to that lawyer for a moment. (The one who asked what he must do to inherit eternal life.)[31] When Jesus told him that he had answered correctly, to "Love God and others," the man, an expert in the law of God, should have replied that it's not possible to fulfill God's law perfectly. Logically, the man should have inquired further.

Love Your Enemy

When it comes to loving one's enemy, let me clarify something here about abusers. I refer to child abusers and those who commit spousal abuse, whether mental or physical. To love others, including enemies, does not mean to accept abuse.

When Jesus expounded on loving our enemies in Matthew 5:44, He didn't mean to submit to physical or sexual abuse. To understand the process, take this verse and go through it carefully. It's important to examine this in detail because evil people twist the Bible's teachings. They do this to gain and keep control over their victims. When Jesus taught to love one's enemy, He meant to forgive them as you would release someone from debt. He did not say enable abusers or look the other way when to do so allows their evil to go unchecked. And Jesus certainly didn't mean to tolerate physical abuse and mental torture.

There is a time and a place to forgive. During abuse is not the time or place. How this works out in everyday life is different according to the circumstances. It depends on a person's ability to intervene or resist a violent offender. Children can hardly protect themselves; they need adult protection. To obey the command to love God and others requires intervention when possible. The level of response depends on the relationship to the victim and or abuser. The best protection may be to call law enforcement and inform them of the abuse. Law enforcement officers in the US are trained to intervene in domestic violence. Studies prove that arresting a violent abuser is the best way to stop the violence. It's not foolproof by any means and the risk of retribution is real.

But the lawyer was there for confrontation and didn't have a repentant heart. In answer to "Love your neighbor as yourself," the lawyer asked Jesus who was his neighbor. Jesus told him the story of the Good Samaritan. It's interesting Jesus used a Samaritan in His story because Jews and Samaritans did not like one another. It was a racial thing. Self-righteous Jews detested Samaritans and looked down upon them as half-breeds. They would call someone a Samaritan as a curse. Once, when wanting to curse Jesus, a group of Pharisees called him a Samaritan and demon-possessed.[32]

Keep this hatred in mind while reading the following account. It gives more meaning to Jesus's use of a Samaritan as the good guy: Jesus told about a man traveling to Jericho who had been assaulted during a violent robbery. He was beaten, stripped of his clothing, and left lying on the roadside half dead. A priest happened by and saw the man lying wounded. He veered to the other side of the road, and doing so passed by the wounded man. Next came a Levite, another religious leader, and he did the same. Jesus named the religious elite and depicted them having no mercy in their hearts, a factor playing into their building hatred of Him.

The third man to come along on the Jericho Road was the Samaritan. He was different. He stopped and in compassion rendered aid to the wounded man. Can you guess the lawyer's gut reaction at hearing this? He and his ilk have been weighed in the balances with Samaritans and found wanting.

Compassion is a vital component of love. Compassion for others involves doing all you can to ease the needs of hurting people. Love for God is revealed to a dying world by how you use resources for others' benefit. Jesus takes notice if you help others when and wherever you can. His loving heart dwells upon every living soul on this earth. Imagine God's pleasure when one of His children helps another child of His. Better yet, when we help an enemy.

The command to love others not only benefits them but also benefits us. Can you imagine God's delight when we forgive our enemies? It may be in Heaven before you realize the benefits of loving others in tangible ways. But, even here, right now, anyone can make a difference in the lives of those in need. If you want to help someone, start by praying for opportunities to get involved. Then go and make a difference.

Where we serve is not the vital point. But listen, it's rare for an opportunity to fall in your lap. It usually takes you making the first step. It is normal to feel reluctant when making plans to change your life, to shift your focus from yourself to others and their needs. Start small. Ease into it. The reward is a sense of purpose.

The references include several trusted ministries to consider.

Actions to Consider

☞ To build the strength needed to forgive someone who harmed you, start with quickly forgiving others for the inconsiderate things they do. As you practice this, you will be in a better position to forgive the worst offenders in your life.

☞ To forgive isn't to condone what others did to you or to excuse them. Forgive for the Lord's sake, then for your good. Remember, on the cross Jesus cried out, "Father, forgive them for they do not know what they do."[33]

Where are you in this? Do you want the love of God poured out on you, so you recognize it? Are you searching for it? If you are, prayer is the way to ask God for all you need to love Him and others. His Spirit helps in the search and helps us when we pray. Jesus also pleads our cause with God, pointing to His wounds to justify our prayers' access to God.

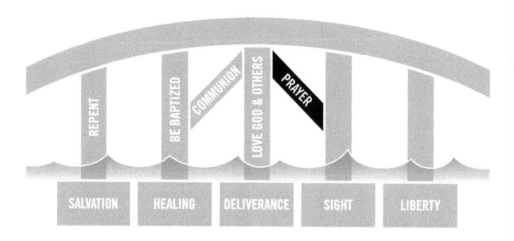

CHAPTER 10

Prayer

"Watch and pray, lest you enter into temptation. The spirit indeed is willing, but the flesh is weak." Matthew 26:41

JESUS PRAYED. HE TOLD HIS FOLLOWERS to pray. That's because it is the means ordained to commune with God. Prayer is more than going through a wish list. To set the tone here, we're to avoid being like those "users" in our lives. You know, the ones who only call or come around when in need. Don't be like that with God.

So, how do we pray in keeping with God's design, and what does God want from us when we pray? Since God created us with a personality, it stands to reason His personality is similar. With all due reverence to God's holiness, He did create us in His likeness. This means God has a friendship-minded desire toward us; He wants to hear from us. Because friends talk to one another, prayer is the best way to come close to God and know Him better.[34]

Want to see an example of this closeness represented by prayer? Turn to John 13:23. In Jesus's day most tables were low, a few inches above floor level. As a result, people sat on the floor, likely on pillows or mats, and leaned on one arm or propped on an elbow to eat. In this passage there is a disciple at the table, one whom Jesus loved, John. He was leaning against Jesus when Jesus announced one of the disciples was going to betray Him. Peter motions for John to ask Jesus who is the betrayer. He has only to look back over his shoulder and whisper the question.

The Apostle Jesus Loved

So what made John's friendship with Jesus different from the others? First, for whatever reason, John was one of Jesus's inner circle. This circle also included John's brother James, and Peter. These three had been fishing partners on Galilee and may have grown up together. Peter's brashness is pretty well known, and James and John had the nicknames Sons of Thunder. It seems Jesus may have surrounded himself with these three for their boldness.

These three were always with Jesus, to the exclusion of other disciples, at times. Jesus took them with Him when He raised Jarius's daughter from the dead. They accompanied him on the mountain when He was transfigured as God Almighty descended on the summit. They were the close by in Gethsemane when Jesus prayed in deep agony until blood seeped from His face. During this anguish, Jesus went for comfort to where Peter, James, and John lay sleeping.

It is an astonishing thought that Jesus needed comfort when He was on earth as a man. And, who's to say He doesn't find comfort in our prayers even now. Not that He needs comforting, but it may be 'comfortable with us' is a decent way to consider it. I have no doubt Jesus enjoys the time we spend in prayer with Him.

This disciple did not ask Jesus if it is him who will betray Him, for his love for Jesus would forbid such a grievous act. John's affection for Jesus was so deep he was the only disciple to stand near the cross during the crucifixion.

How to pray is simple. Tell God if you need help. One of the best prayers in the Bible is when David cried out to God, "Help, Lord..." Spurgeon called it a "remarkable prayer." Another short effective prayer is when Peter cried out, "Lord, save me!" as he sank in stormy waves. Prayer needn't be complicated to have power with Jesus. A woman whose daughter was demon-possessed once came to Jesus, begging help. When He first ignored her (to test her faith), she kept crying, "Lord, help me!" Then the Son of God rewarded her for persistent trust.

Prayer is a supernatural link to God. He wants to hear your prayers.

So, why is praying so hard? I went online to see if I could find any single cause as the reason prayer can be hard. I found this principle and know it is true:

Praying itself isn't hard. Persistence in praying is hard. That is not surprising considering all the distractions in life. It's like one author said, "Just do it."

Before looking at ways to 'just do it,' here are some common hindrances to praying:

⚠ Sin, especially willful, known sin.

⚠ Broken relationships. The times I'm hateful to my wife hinders my prayers and hinders God from giving what I asked.

⚠ An unforgiving or judgmental attitude. A condemning spirit. A mindset of fault-finding rooted in pride.

⚠ Unbelief hinders prayer. Do you like it when people don't believe you? Such as when told you'll do something for them?

⚠ Falling victim to false teachings like 'name-it-and-claim-it' sets you up for failure. I fell for this false doctrine early in my Christian life. It may be worth taking a moment to read this endnote.[35]

⚠ Spiritual warfare: This is a tough one to recognize. Not to blame everything on the devil, but there are times when hindered prayer is satanic influence. Don't focus on rebuking Satan or his forces, but rather pray for protection from all evil, and ask God to cover your loved ones and you in the power of the blood of Christ. The blood of Jesus guards you in spiritual warfare.

☞ Another safeguard: keep the relationship with God right by having a short account of sin. A repentant willingness on your part is a good defense when praying for people caught in bondage.

To overcome hindrances to prayer, put in place a habit of prayer. A special location dedicated for prayer is ideal when possible.

To maintain a habit of prayer, use a list containing the names and needs of family and friends. I use a 3x5 card when there is an urgent need for prayer throughout the day and keep it in a pocket.

Writing prayer requests on the bathroom mirror with dry-erase is a great reminder. If you practice writing your prayers somewhere enough times, a habit will develop. A good thing about developing a prayer-habit is when you skip, you'll notice.

In 1st Thessalonians 5:17 Paul exhorts us to pray continually. What does it mean? For one, it's mindful of conversation with God, Jesus, and the Holy Spirit throughout the day. Talk to Him, or Them, as you would any other friend. When I first started doing this it felt weird, like talking to the imaginary friend I had when a kid. But Spurgeon and others teach that we can put ourselves in God's presence by faith. The result of using one's imagination based on faith is not the same as imaginary. Praying like this relies upon the truth portraying God as an affectionate Father; Jesus, as a tender brother and friend; the Holy Spirit as a devoted comforter. Through prayer, you visit them throughout the day.

Spurgeon suggests using your mind's eye to picture being in the throne-room with God and visualize yourself standing close and talking to Him. Insulate yourself from distractions, and in that quiet moment, go to Heaven in your mind and pray. Sound crazy? It may be, but in a right way. It takes crazy faith to believe all the Bible teaches about God and Heaven.

When you choose to believe God is who the Bible declares Him to be and that He wants you to know Him, feelings toward prayer will change. It strengthens your faith when you pray as if you are in His very presence. At this point faith should be all or nothing, for it takes persistent, stubborn faith to prevail in prayer.

So what results should be prayed for, what outcome do you want to happen? First, what you pray for must be God's will. There are volumes written on knowing the will of God. Without going into that kind of depth, God's will for the most part is spelled out in the Bible. The Ten Commandments are an example. Then look at Jesus's teachings in the New Testament. These will sift your desires if you are not sure they line up with God's approval.

Let me warn you: do not dictate to God how He should carry out answering your prayers. Even with good intentions it's easy to boss God by telling Him how to do what you want. Bossing God around doesn't work. The point is try not to tell God what to do. Rather, ask Him to give whatever you need and let God do it—His way. He knows best how to answer.

In Isaiah 55:8–9, God described His ways and thoughts as not being not like ours. And how His thoughts and methods are much higher than ours, as high as the heavens are above the earth. Taking this into account, I recognize some of my prayers have unrealistic expectations. Unrealistic prayer sets me up for disappointment.

Realistic prayer thanks God for everyday mercies. Because it's easy to take for granted having a decent place to live, food, clothing, and good health, among other things. Writing "Be Thankful" on a card carried with us keeps us from ingratitude.

Before ending this chapter, let's look at what is generally called "The Lord's Prayer."

Our Father in heaven,

Hallowed be Your name.

Your kingdom come.

Your will be done

On earth as it is in Heaven.

Give us this day our daily bread.

And forgive us our debts,

As we forgive our debtors.

And lead us not into temptation,

But deliver us from the evil one.

For yours is the kingdom and the power

and the glory forever.

Jesus gave this prayer as an example of worship, not as a mindless repetition. It is instructive, even beautiful when sung. Max Lucado believes the essential aspect of prayer is "an awareness of God as your Father." The first portion of this model prayer is directed to God, the second portion to personal needs, and the third for protection from Satan (Note the use of the word "our" throughout the prayer.)

I have prayed through this example at times when overwhelmed, line by line, lingering on each point with additional petitions added.

An example of focusing on one aspect is the phrase, "Hallowed be Your name." It means "may God's name be reverenced, or respected." His name is who He is—in the Hebrew, LORD means the self-existent one, uncreated, Supreme Being. How I act, where I go, what I look at, and how I treat others, even how I treat my body, can show reverence to God. All these things affect my life as a Christian and also others around me, whether they respect God or scorn Him is no matter. Use this prayer as a guide if you like, or pray it as written. Only keep in mind prayer doesn't have to be so formal all the time.

It is not required to have a prayer chapel or altar in the home or a prayer rug. While these kinds of things are not necessary, location can help. I like praying on a mountaintop, but God hears me just as well in traffic.

While visiting Israel years ago, I stood at the Wailing Wall and prayed. I expected to experience God in some unique way. I wore a tallit (prayer shawl) to set the tone and prayed for several minutes. Nothing happened. I prayed some more. Nothing. I asked God, "What's going on?" His reply, "I'm not here any more so than any other place. I live in your heart and am always with you." Hmmm. Bummer. Not bummer God is with me. It was that I traveled a long ways to have an exceptional experience praying at the Wailing Wall. God to David: location doesn't matter so much. Check.

So I looked around from under the tallit and listened to the voices of the faithful Jews praying. It was a lamenting sound, the men rocking back and forth crying to God.

The important point of location is limiting distractions.

Actions to Consider

Praying the Scriptures is very powerful because it is praying God's Word back to Him. Here are a few examples of verses paraphrased as a personal appeal to God:

- Psalm 32:8: "Instruct me and teach me in the way I should go, guide me with Your eye."
- Psalm 50:15: "I call upon You in my day of trouble; deliver me, I will glorify You."
- Ephesians 1:17–18: "Give me the spirit of wisdom and revelation in the knowledge of You, the eyes of my understanding being enlightened; that I may know what is the hope of Your calling..."
- Ephesians 3:16–19: "Give me, according to the riches of Your glory, strength and might through Your Spirit in my mind and soul, that Jesus may dwell in my heart through faith; that I, being rooted and grounded in love, may comprehend the width, length, depth, and height—to experience the love of Christ..."
- Philippians 1:9–11: "Expand my love in knowledge and discernment, that I may approve the excellent things, that I may be sincere and without offense till the day of Christ, and fill me with the fruits of righteousness by Jesus, to Your glory and praise."
- Philippians 4:13: "I can do all things through Christ who strengthens me."
- Colossians 1:9–11: "Fill me with the knowledge of Your will in all wisdom and spiritual understanding; that I may walk worthy of You, Lord, fully pleasing You, being fruitful in every good work, and increasing in the knowledge of You; strengthen me with all might, according to Your glorious power, so I may have all patience in long-suffering, with joy."

You may also say someone else's name in your place. Not only in these verses, but also pray other Psalms inserting personal applications.

Give God time in prayer. He is waiting to hear from you.

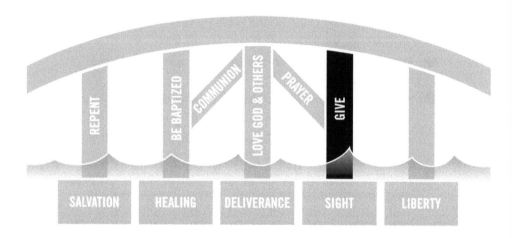

REPENT · BE BAPTIZED · COMMUNION · LOVE GOD & OTHERS · PRAYER · GIVE

SALVATION · HEALING · DELIVERANCE · SIGHT · LIBERTY

CHAPTER 11

Give

"Give, and it will be given to you: good measure, pressed down, shaken together, and running over will be put into your bosom. For with the same measure that you use, it will be measured back to you." Luke 6:38

To GIVE AS TAUGHT IN THE Bible means giving to God's work, and the easiest way, of course, is to give money. Money comes to mind when the word give is used within a religious context. It's reasonable to associate money with that teaching, but is that it? Give money and be done with the requirement to contribute as the Bible teaches?

Surely not.

If you're struggling financially and can barely pay the bills each month, relax. More than money is available to give; there are times when money can be a worthless gift in God's estimation.[36]

For one thing, God doesn't need money. He uses gold as pavement in Heaven.[37] The following story makes a good point: an angel tells a man he is going to die soon and to pack one suitcase with his most treasured possessions and bring it to Heaven with him. So the man packs and then he dies. At the pearly gate Peter meets him and says to him, "Welcome, put your suitcase there on the table, open it, let's see what you've got." The man opens the case. Peter looks up, surprised, and asks, "You brought pavement?"

[Come on. You know that's funny.]

When someone gives in the Biblical sense, God looks at the heart to see their motive. Is the gift given freely, or stingily? Anything given grudgingly to God and His kingdom work doesn't count much with God, for He loves a cheerful giver.[38]

Giving is also sharing with others in need. Money is rarely the answer when it comes to individuals in need, so there is a caution here. Money management may be the real problem with someone in need. By that I mean many Christians in this country, myself included, have a lack of discipline when it comes to spending habits. So, if we give money to someone undisciplined with their spending habits, it does them no good. Whereas, arranging that person's attendance in a money management seminar, with their consent, of course, is a good way to give. You could even pay for the sessions, but again, this warrants caution. The principle is those needing help with finances should invest in their success of becoming debt-free by paying for the course.

My wife and I attended a Dave Ramsey course a few years back. The need came about because when I retired, my spending remained the same as when I had been on a full salary. This careless practice went on for several years without me noticing. This was because I didn't monitor my savings account, which was linked to checking. Then, the light came on when I happened to check my savings and saw the balance had dropped significantly.

I did a quick income vs. expenses and discovered I was in the red $250 per month. Simple math, but I hadn't taken the time to discipline myself and live by a budget adjusted to my reduced income, and I wasn't living extravagantly. The only debt obligations I had was paying half the mortgage and for a Harley I had purchased when I retired. So, I assumed all was well.

Our church offered the Dave Ramsey course about that time. After looking into it, Kris and I signed up. In the first or second session, we did a worksheet to determine our total short-term debt. It totaled $46,000. This amount was unbelievable. It included her truck payment, my Harley payment, and our credit cards...$46,000. The course moderator said it only takes most people 30 months to become debt-free, excluding any mortgage. I didn't believe it and said so. He explained that for this program to work I had to trust the principles involved for they were proven to work. Okay then.

During the next few days, I mulled over the figures. The object was to cut debt, however possible. It proved emotionally painful when I realized the Harley had to go. I sold it soon after and cut $12,000 of debt, and, in the process, saved $355 per month.

> *[A little side note about riders and their motorcycles: it's easy to become emotionally attached to those machines. I think it's because of the freedom and adventure they offer. When I left that Harley at the dealer to sell on consignment, it felt like leaving my dog at the pound. I'm not saying it makes sense, just saying it happens, and to make the point: money has emotional energy.]*

We made other cutbacks. Like only going out once each month to eat out. And by other small savings here and there were soon in the black a few hundred dollars each month. Now, there's more involved in the process as far as the payment structures and so forth. But the bottom line is, after exactly 30 months we were debt-free concerning that $46,000.

I told this to make a point: being free of consumer debt now enables us to give more of ourselves by having the funds to do so. It works out like this:

Many opportunities await someone wanting to help others. Many of those in need are waiting for that help. However, there are costs involved, unless you're donating time locally, and this is perfectly fine if that's where you serve. But if there comes a time you want to take giving to a different level, if you're debt-free, the options broaden. Like traveling to another country to help out short-term. Typically, you must cover costs for travel and living expenses. The ministries I've served with overseas covered a few in-country costs with the limited funds they had, and I provided the rest. This method is how most short-term service works.

Now, I've heard the argument and even asked myself the same: wouldn't it be better to send the money overseas instead of going? There are two sides to this argument. One is the Christian-vacation mindset of going abroad. Those who go for the travel are known as vacationaries. My first overseas experience was as a vacationary. Even then, the ensuing experience opened my eyes and heart to an area of giving I never knew existed.

So, back to money. Whether you spend funds while serving or send monetary support for those on the front lines, money is a tool when used rightly.

Now, remember, this book is a guide to restoration of confidence and not intended to pull you down. Part of restoring hopefulness involves regaining a sense of purpose. Giving is an easy way to feel a sense of purpose, even a reason to exist. Meaningful life comes out of the fact your existence is valuable and you matter to those you help. There is someone out in the world today who needs you.

Even if all you can do is pray, find a need somewhere and give yourself in prayer for that person involved.

For those not called to serve abroad or in their home country: it's easy to help support those called to leave their homeland.

Come on, let's make a difference. Give.

Elizabeth Seaton said, "Live simply so others may simply live."

Here is a ministry I've worked with and support, if you need a starting place: www.kupendwaministries.org/donate

As I wrap up this chapter it feels good thinking about the potential impact of each one of you. You can make a difference in the life of someone hurting. If you're considering how you may give, thank you. And thanks also to all who provide support already.

One last thought about money, please. Money doesn't power God's work in the world; it's but a cog in the machinery. God's love fuels His work through prayer. Our place in this economy is putting the effort to give, how and where needed.

Actions to Consider

☞ Pray about what you're able to do—make a list.

☞ Search for ministries serving others. Make sure they are Christ-centered by giving priority to sharing the Gospel. Reasonable operating costs deducted by ministries are 5%-10%.

☞ Set a date by which you will give something, somehow, somewhere. If you write it somewhere, you'll be reminded daily to take action.

☞ If, or when, you are involved with supporting a ministry, correspond with them, encourage them besides monetary support.

☞ See if they will send pictures of the work, the staff, and the people they're serving. Pics are a great reminder to pray.

Giving is a way to teach the world what a Christian looks like in action.

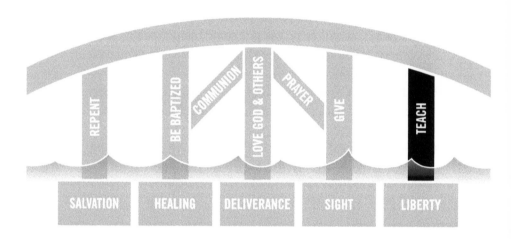

CHAPTER 12

Teach

Also known as "Make Disciples"

"Go therefore and make disciples of all the nations, baptizing them in the name of the Father and of the Son and of the Holy Spirit, teaching them to observe all things that I have commanded you;" Matthew 28:19

ONE EVENING, AS I SAT IN the sergeant's office at police headquarters, the chief stopped by. He told me to apply for an upcoming instructor's course. My stomach knotted. He already had me scheduled to teach recruits in the academy a class on explosives recognition. At the time, I was a newly promoted sergeant just learning the ropes. I was on the bomb squad and knew the subject matter, but taking on this course during the first few weeks of promotion was bad timing for my part. The instructor's course was infamous; reputed to be the hardest course in local law enforcement training. Additionally, I feared public speaking.

The course deserved its reputation. Without going into the difficulties encountered, I passed. A few weeks later, I taught my first class. It was amazing. I loved it and now enjoy teaching. Years later, when asked to teach a men's class at church, I agreed and taught for a year. I still teach whenever I can. It's hard to describe the enjoyment of sharing knowledge in a classroom setting.

The thought of making disciples, however, makes me shrink back. When Jesus gave the command called "The Great Commission," He gave us a huge task. But Jesus showed us the way. He poured

His life into those who followed Him, teaching them the ways and rules of kingdom living. He expects us to do the same. So let's look at teaching as a practical way to share the hope we have, with others.

Jesus's disciples told all who listened about His resurrection from the dead. The resurrection was the catalyst that changed them from cowards to men and women filled with hope and courage. Even now, new Christians need help to understand all of Jesus's teaching and how to apply that teaching in everyday life. Prioritizing Jesus's teachings reveals the Gospel message is the most important lesson.

It's easy for Christians to lose the awe and wonder of the Gospel, so I'm going to revisit it here. Try reading through the following brief Biblical history with a fresh look, as if the first time.

The human race has experienced every conceivable form of evil. Our brutal history is one of war, rape, plundering, slavery, torture, and murder. This violence all began when Cain killed Abel. Apart from any positive influence God has had on a people, the history of our planet is dark and depressing.

Read accounts of ancient military campaigns conducted by various kingdoms and empires. The utter brutalities of conquering armies against those they vanquished defy belief. It's a wonder that civilization survived thus far.

Cruelty seems innate within the human heart. Without teachings about morals, the value of human life, and the rule of law, murder rules. It's right below the surface of every society today. People kill for pleasure, for vengeance, and to steal, among other things. The list goes on ad nauseam.

Early in human history, when mayhem broke out, what did God do? He destroyed the earth with a devastating flood. What did He intend to teach us about this event, the event that wiped out the human race with the exception of eight people? Did we, the human race, learn the lesson? We know we didn't. Centuries of dominant evil go by. Later, enlightened societies developed rules of law. And still those societies could not resist the evil coming from within their people. Even the Roman Empire, the greatest empire to exist, fell from within. What happened to them? The people responsible to teach their children failed. They did not impart the knowledge and necessity of values and morals.

Into the darkness and misery of human history during Roman rule, the Son of God came. Born a babe who spent His first night in a stable. The Apostle John writes, "In Him was life, and the life was the light of men. And the light shines in the darkness…"[39]

When Jesus came of age, He went about teaching. His teachings changed human history. Western democracies resulted from the Judeo-Christian values. These values are incorporated into the laws and structures of these governments, and now there exists a primary division of nations. The division is between those nations with the teachings of Christ as the bedrock of their laws, as opposed to nations with a record of human rights violations. You need but ask people living in these countries if this is true.

During Jesus's brief ministry, He taught that He would conquer death. He meant not only to conquer eternal death of the body and soul but also to conquer the death of our hopes and dreams. He taught that He had come to give abundant life in place of death.[40]

This abundant life Jesus promised is spiritual abundance. At times it includes physical abundance, but that isn't guaranteed. In this life even good Christians suffer. The principle of suffering is necessary to understanding how God works. We must teach this when teaching discipleship (how to live like Jesus). It is only fair to warn new Christians: they will experience their share of hardships and heartbreaks. Jesus was known as a Man of suffering and He taught that His followers also would suffer. A blessing comes to mind to help us endure suffering. It is the peace of knowing when the body dies the Christian wakes in Heaven. Believing this alleviates fear of death to a certain extent. And belief comes with a blessing: the knowledge that your life matters to God even though you may feel like a failure. God values your life, and what you do here counts in eternity. When you allow this truth to give hope, it strengthens you and your life will teach others by example.

As far as spiritual strength goes, it develops over time with experiences of hardships. Remain faithful to the teachings of Christ to the best of your ability and endure suffering; strength will develop. (Working out with weights teaches this principle in the physical realm.)

A disciple needs lessons of perseverance taught along with a few other factors of the Christian life. They deserve to know what will help them endure and how to have hope. If seasoned Christians won't take the time to teach them these things, who will?

There is another way I should mention: pastoral teaching of sound Biblical doctrine. Other means include classes at church. But let's take a look at different ways we all can teach on an informal level.

So far, this chapter has covered formal discipleship requirements that Jesus had in mind when He said His followers were to go out and make disciples.

But where does everyday teaching play a part in Jesus's command? Have you ever considered yourself as a teacher? In a way, we all are, of sorts. What lessons are you imparting at work? How about in traffic, what are you teaching other drivers? And I don't mean sign language. What about parents? Parents know they are teachers. A good parent teaches innumerable lessons throughout the life of a young child. They may even be able to show a teenager a thing or two. You never know. Take a moment if you're a parent and think about the lessons you're imparting. Be strong; it is my belief that every lesson taught a child requires exponentially more times explaining why.

Yet another method of teaching, one that God uses for the stubborn among us, is the rod of discipline.[41]

Now I know the subject of physical discipline is a much-debated topic today. First, Jesus does not teach anyone to beat a child. Beatings from which bruises or bleeding result are child abuse and illegal. That kind of mistreatment is the criminal extreme. It is not what the Bible teaches about loving discipline. I do believe physical discipline reinforces to a child the need for compliance to rules. This applies to rules of a household or those of society at large. Absence of discipline that is fair, consistent, and loving, accounts for youth detention centers filled with juveniles.

The rod mentioned in Proverbs 3:24 may be thought of as a switch (a thin branch from a bush), as in "getting a switching." Ever get switched? I did. It only took one switching from our housekeeper when I was four years old to stop me from chasing after my mother as she drove off to work.

To discipline a child is to teach them. It's done out of love. If a two-year-old unlocks the front door and sneaks out to play in a busy street, what to do? The child's life is in danger. Talking to the child doesn't work. What if spanking that child results in the child obeying? Is the comparatively minor pain a fair exchange to prevent crippling injury or death? The question is rhetorical, the answer obvious.

It's teaching the philosophy of discipline at issue here. It's about adults having the responsibility to teach their children about the dangers of certain behaviors. Destructive behaviors in the life of a child, when not confronted by authority, will lead to problems as an adult. It's the "cause and effect" rule of life. The lack of loving discipline accounts for much of the criminal behavior of juveniles on the evening news nightly. Note that I said loving discipline, not sadistic abuse. Adults subjected to cruel abuse as children may account for half the crimes committed.

Discipline is an act of love when it teaches a lesson to protect from harm. What about parents who say they love their child too much to punish them? Failing to teach a child to stay away from fire, is this love?

To teach a child a sense of entitlement by giving them everything they want, is this love? How are they going to make their way in the world when they leave home? Parents, are you teaching sound rules about work? How about the financial principle to cultivate savings to purchase what they want?

I've seen plenty of adults struggling due to the absence of parental teaching early in their lives. They are children in adult bodies, and they make some of the most outrageous and immature decisions causing all sorts of mayhem. Then, the devastating effect ripples down through succeeding generations. All stemming from a lack of decent parental teaching. If you experienced a void of knowledge from your parents, break the cycle with your children.[42]

These are enough negative examples, maybe too many. For that, I apologize. To end this chapter on a positive note, please consider the uplifting effect of teaching. Share life's lessons learned and share based on concern and love for others. Love teaches in order to protect. As we teach, we also learn.

As for me, one final lesson I want to share in this chapter is that of the turtle on a fencepost. What does a turtle on a fence post teach me? Want the answer, or figure it out yourself? Look here[43] to see if you got it right.

This chapter completes Step Two. If you worked through the preceding chapters, well done! The upright portions of the bridge structure now rest on the foundations of Step One. In the final section of this book, Step Three, the span and deck of the bridge are put into place one plank at a time.

For you who are practicing the principles presented so far, you are on top of the bridge diagram. To see yourself like that means you are lifted above that dark roiling water pictured on the cover.

You are on your way to freedom, though it may not feel like it yet, but you are making progress. And the best is coming.

I find the next section exciting because we examine the way the Holy Spirit gives aspects of His life to us. These aspects are called Fruit of the Spirit.

Step Three

Moving in the Spirit—
Fruit of the Spirit

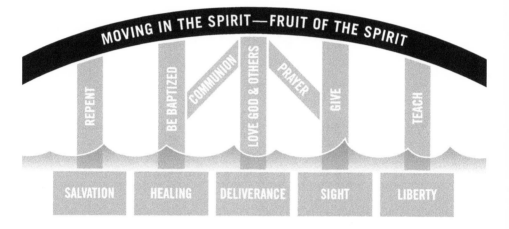

Moving in the Spirit—Fruit of the Spirit

"If we live in the Spirit, let us also walk in the Spirit." Paul in Galatians 5:25

KEEP THIS DEFINITION IN MIND: THE Greek word for walk is "proof of ability, being occupied with something, to live a certain way."

The span in the image opposite overarches the top of your spiritual bridge to represent the work of the Holy Spirit. This span crosses the top of each pier structure. It rests on the upright principles of the Seven Commands. These in turn rest on the foundational promises. Remember, this is all analogous.

One last step now remains. Placing the fruit (virtues) of the Spirit as planks. This is decking on the span, and on these virtues, you walk on the bridge of spiritual freedom. To put the span in place, you must yield to the influence of the Holy Spirit. Yielding is the natural outpouring of obeying the Seven Commands of Jesus.

The planks represent fruit, listed in Galatians 5:22–24. The analogy of fruit is the evidence of good works.

Several years ago, I meandered through a vineyard. I walked up and down rows of vines hanging with clusters of grapes. I don't know what enriched the growth of these particular grapes, but whatever it was, the evidence hung everywhere. Each vine came up out of the soil and spread out to the sides, clinging to supporting wires.

Branches were tangled with those of other vines, the leaves facing up and out to the sun. No matter how far I walked, and it was a big vineyard, clusters of grapes hung heavy.

This is a picture of a person walking in the Spirit. Pruned by God from destructive habits, and as a branch, drawing life from the Vine, Jesus. I saw why He used the analogy of a vineyard in John Chapter 15.

There are other aspects, or fruit, of the Spirit in every life lived according to God's teachings. The nine listed in Galatians form a core pattern to look for. You may also live by, walk in, and use them as markers of progress along the way. These nine are listed here, and each one will be examined in subsequent chapters.

- Love
- Joy
- Peace
- Patience
- Kindness
- Goodness
- Faithfulness
- Gentleness
- Self-control

These nine aspects of fruit are interconnected. Paul separated them to give us examples we could recognize. They have a logical sequence when considering Love should be first. It seems as if each attribute, or virtue, flows out of the preceding one. However, God in His sovereignty and wisdom may bring a different order of these virtues into your life as He heals you. You're in a process. Be open to the fruit popping up in everyday life. In this sense, it's also an adventure, one God orchestrates.

If you're ready to start walking, a bridge for your troubled soul waits to carry you above the dark waters of despair. The cover of this book conveys the experience.

MOVING IN THE SPIRIT—FRUIT OF THE SPIRIT

Placing the Span on Which to Walk

"I am the Vine, you are the branches. He who abides in Me, and I in him, bears much fruit; for without Me you can do nothing." John 15:3

HAVE YOU READ JOHN 15? IF so, did you notice in verse two Jesus said every branch in Him that does not bear fruit he takes away? This is important: in Greek it means 'to lift.' When the verse reads 'take away,' it means take a vine and move it up from lying in the dirt. Lift it back where it belongs—in the sunlight. If you are close to giving up, it means "to restore to usefulness, to enable one to find purpose." Using logic here is most helpful. When Jesus said every branch in Him, He meant His child. A Christian. One adopted into the family of God with his or her name written in the Lamb's Book of Life. A drooping branch is one downtrodden by life, depressed, wounded either emotionally, mentally, or both.

God keeps watch over His vineyard, which symbolizes His people. He lifts every branch hanging down in the dirt. I reiterate here because it's imperative to grasp this. God lifts the fallen branch and cleans off the grime and filth. Then, with tender love, places it (the fallen Christian) back up where it receives sunlight. He wants that branch, meaning you, to thrive and bear fruit. It pictures restoration.

How do I know this for sure? Look at verse three of John 15 – Jesus said, "you," meaning those he is talking to were already clean.

Remember the Passover? He washed the disciples' feet. These are the same ones He taught during the Last Supper and while doing so said they were clean except for their feet. The analogy intended is that when walking in the world, sin dirties the Christian's appearance. Sin must be confessed and forsaken to wash and remain clean spiritually.

Verse three revealed the restorative power of the words Jesus spoke.[44] God's Word has a cleansing effect, and when you obey His Word, it places you in a position to bear fruit in life. The two are inseparable: cleanliness and obedience.

Going on to verse 4 gives the beautiful promise: abiding or living according to His teachings brings fruit. Virtue results from any life lived close to the Son of God. It is inevitable. If you cannot bear the thought of having yet another thing requiring effort, please allow this to encourage you: God produces the fruit. This means He provides you opportunities to do good to others (Fruit = good works). All you have to do is abide and rest in the Savior's presence. Then respond as occasions present themselves.

Now, verse six describes the branch that does not abide in Christ. This one is not His. It is cast out and withers. This is symbolic of synthetic Christians. These people die outside the protection of Jesus's Atonement. Although they gave intellectual assent, they stopped short of committing their lives to His rule. Jesus said these branches are gathered and burned. It is the fate of all who die without their names in the Book of Life. Their end is eternal fire.[45]

As for us, walking (abiding) in the Spirit and living the Christian life is a lifelong process. Walking on a bridge above despairing issues does not keep us from all storms of life. Even upon a bridge, hurricane winds may batter. A despairing wave may reach up and inundate you. But for all who stand in God's freedom they no longer drown in despair. Instead, they stand firm.

Let the winds blow as they will; those winds will eventually die down. Any wave that washes up drains away, for all storms do subside. Looking ahead are markers of progress on the span. These are the virtues of the Spirit. We see them becoming evident in everyday life. The virtues are not only planks upon which to stand and walk, but their presence is a sign of being on the right path. Life becomes more than empty suffering. We have decent effects of change occurring, changes others enjoy when around us. Bearing Christian fruit gives purpose to life, that crucial element of hope.

Even a storm drenched branch bears fruit. It is inevitable because the ability to bear fruit is always the work of God's Spirit. Life tests us with storms, there's no doubt. When battered about and weary with it all, let the feelings be what they will. If it hurts, let it hurt. No matter the emotions right now, it's okay to be real. It's part of being human and God is never surprised. However, when God's fruit is in the heart, Christians who walk in the Spirit will always have evidence of that walk.

Walk forward into your future and see the aspects of fruit waiting for you.

LOVE

MOVING IN THE SPIRIT—FRUIT OF THE SPIRIT

CHAPTER 13

Love

"And now abide faith, hope, love, these three; but the greatest of these is love." 1 Corinthians 13:13

REMEMBER, BIBLICAL FRUIT IS AN ANALOGY for good works. Love as a verb is placed first in Galatians 5:22 for a reason. The other fruits flow from and remain intertwined with love. The word for love in Galatians is the Greek word agape. It means affection and benevolence. It is the most profound sort of love—the very same love God has for you. Even then it doesn't come close to describing the depth, breadth, height, or sheer quality of this level of love. How could it? Love is God's essence.

Our love is at the level of agapao meaning love in a social or moral sense. There is a vast difference between agape love and agapao. As I write this, Valentine's Day is a week away. An example comes to mind about the difference between God's love for us and our ordinary love for Him. It's like the difference between romance for a sweetheart and affection for a friend, but, even that doesn't do the meaning justice.

God's love for you exceeds the best feelings of love you've ever had for someone, even that of a mother's love for a precious child. God's love for you remains constant no matter how bad you feel about yourself. He loves you with the deepest affection imaginable. The proof is the way God loves in the verb sense and acts on your behalf, every time.

His love ensures you have His undivided attention when you pray. He understands what you feel. He comprehends every detail involved in whatever you are going through. His love is the reason Romans 8:28 stands sure. This is because that promise is founded on God's immovable, unchangeable, never-ending love for you. It is a rock-solid foundation of love.

Consider, then, the fruit of love is an outflow of God's very own nature.[46] Do you want this kind of love to fill you and flow from you? There is something you must do. First of all, look back over the commands of Jesus in Step Two. Ensure you have obeyed the first two commands. If so, make sure you are striving daily to obey the others with the best of your abilities. Perfection isn't required—it's not even possible—but you do have to give it a go. If you are striving to keep His commandments, then you are abiding in His love, regardless of whether you feel it or not. This is a good opportunity to practice living by faith.

Second: As you obey His commands and abide in His love, the fruit of love flows out of you. Jesus bears responsibility for this since He assigned us the task to bear fruit. By the way, fruit remains for eternity. Our eternal rewards stem from the good works, the fruit. When we pray and ask God to give us a fruitful life, Jesus said we'll have it.

It is necessary to ask for God's level of love because without His help we have only social love for others. Don't be shy to ask; be bold. God wants to give the essence of His nature to us. When He gives, it's not ours to keep, but for us to give away.

Now, the exciting part of writing this came when I realized God's love has two straightforward elements—affection and benevolence. We have these already in some measure. The difference is we usually limit who receives our fondnes and benevolence. Let's look at this a little closer.

Benevolence is the key to understanding how to exhibit divine love to others. Benevolence is when you wish the best for others, to be kind and do good to them instead of what they deserve. Jesus put it another way when He said to "do unto others as we would have them do unto us."

We limit benevolence because of conditions we set. As a result, we love conditionally. I'm not talking about the practice of safe boundaries; rather, it's about willingness to do away with conditions and do good for others, regardless. To show benevolence without conditions requires a change in mindset. This is where the work comes in. Changing habitual thoughts and behaviors is difficult, so don't underestimate the process. It's challenging because most of us operate throughout the day on autopilot. By the way, most "Actions to Consider" so far in this book are examples of breaking out of the autopilot habit.

To counter the natural human trait of giving conditional love requires stubborn faith. It is normal to withdraw from those for whom you have no natural affinity. They are the ones who rub you the wrong way. They are the opposite of the things you like. And I'm not talking about trying to have loving feelings for everyone who irks us, so relax. The benevolence of love is an action, something we do, but may not feel like doing.

Want to try it and see what happens? Take a look at 1 Corinthians 13:4–7. Write these verses down on a 3x5 card. Next, think of people you know at work, church, or school who are annoying to be around. Write their names on the same card. Put the card in a work-clothes pocket so you'll have it easily accessible. Now, make a point to say or do something decent for that person. It's okay if all you can manage at the moment is a slight smile, a nod, or a wave of the hand. If you do wave, use all your fingers.

Not allowed are grunting, sighing, rolling the eyes, or leaving the break room when he comes in. At such a point, resist joining in when coworkers run this person down. See if this helps: try thinking about this person's life away from work. What's going on at home with the family? What did this person go through in childhood? Maybe it caused the personality flaw that chaps your hide. It may help you gain a different point of view if you ask yourself: is it possible you, too, ruffle someone else's feathers without even knowing it?[47] May I help with the answer? I bet you do. So do I.

Jesus gave us plenty of examples of how to love the unlovable. He didn't just sit on the throne of Heaven and sing poetic love sonnets to the human race. He loved us action-style. Love moved the Father to send His Son, the Warrior King, down to earth to conduct a rescue campaign. Death had laid claim to every living soul and demanded a ransom. In John 15:13, Jesus said there is no greater love than to lay down your life for another, so He laid His down.

Laying down your life in love can involve more than dying. The idea is sacrificial—doing what is necessary to love someone by acting on their behalf, for their benefit.

Actions to Consider

☞ In keeping with 1 Corinthians 13, how can you show love today?

☞ Who can you show love to, if only to write a letter? Email is okay, but a handwritten note carries more weight.

Look at this, then we'll move on to joy: to love in the manner of Biblical examples is to be like God. Being like God brings you to the restoration of living close to God. This happens within an adoring relationship, and being close to God brings joy.

LOVE

JOY

MOVING IN THE SPIRIT—FRUIT OF THE SPIRIT

CHAPTER 14

Joy

"With everlasting joy on their heads, They shall obtain joy and gladness; Sorrow and sighing shall flee away." Isaiah 51:11b

THE GREEK USE OF JOY IN the New Testament is described in Strong's concordance as calm delight. Yet again, this is another mindset; a choice made if you want joy despite circumstances. Have you known the feeling of joy recently?

In the New Testament joy is something experienced as a result of the following:

- *i* From belief or faith in God's commands, promises, His grace and mercy, for example.
- *i* From something seen, a good deed done well, the faithfulness of others, God's work in your life, a soul saved, to name a few.
- *i* Results of faith, answered prayer, the safety of a loved one, understanding of Scripture, especially of a difficult passage (e.g., Jesus taught that anyone coming to Him—in submission, to serve—who did not hate their loved ones and even their own life could not be His disciple[48]) or from something received. It may be a lesson received through suffering, either from chastening or trials. Endurance comes to mind. To endure hardship and see it through to conclusion or resolution enables one to have joy, if one believes all things work together for good. It could be that someone does a good thing for us and we receive it as the gift intended.

❶ Something done for God (Charitable work, feeding the hungry, supporting an orphanage, supplying water filters to remote villages, and other acts done for the Glory of God or in obedience to His commands).

Joy is different from happiness, and I want to examine the difference. James wrote, "My brethren, count it all joy when you fall into various trials, knowing that the testing of your faith produces patience." (James 4:1–2)

In this verse James used joy in conjunction with being tested and used it instead of the word happiness. Why? Happiness depends on delightful circumstances, whereas joy may remain even during pain-filled times. I don't want to split semantic hairs here about definitions. I make a distinction between happiness and joy only to recognize how to cultivate the latter. It is possible to seize joy despite feeling bad, if you know how to spot it.

I used to think joy and pain were mutually exclusive. Surely, to have joy one must get rid of depression, agony, sadness, or similar emotions that would seem to be in opposition to joy, but it's not that way. Joy is a choice. An example of this choice is in Acts 16:22–25, when Paul and Silas were illegally arrested, beaten without a trial, bound in stocks, and locked up in a local jail. The Biblical account describes the scene.

Acts 16:22-25

Then the multitude rose up together against them; and the magistrates tore off their clothes and commanded them to be beaten with rods. And when they had laid many stripes on them, they threw them into prison, commanding the jailer to keep them securely. Having received such a charge, he put them into the inner prison and fastened their feet in the stocks. But at midnight Paul and Silas were praying and singing hymns to God, and the prisoners were listening to them.

Why did Paul and Silas sing while injured and their feet held in stocks? Circumstances demanded a reaction other than singing. But consider this: Jesus taught in the Beatitudes (Matthew 5:12) that rejoicing is the correct response to suffering and pain. This principle is reiterated by the Apostles. Peter (Acts 5:41,

1 Peter 1:6, 4:13), Paul (Colossians 1:1, 24) and James (James 1:2). With this in mind, it's reasonable to believe Paul had cause to sing. And not only from his duty to obey Scripture, but from prior experiences of worshiping God regardless of circumstances.

Being in pain and bound to prevent movement, Paul still had the freedom to choose his reaction, either rant and rave or have a joyful mindset. To make this choice, he needed to draw from information. A truth he had learned in the past helped him decide his future actions when in the presence of suffering and pain. What knowledge would that be? If you read every chapter in this book leading up to this one, you will have the same awareness.

Paul's knowledge allowed the power of joy to overcome pain from the beating. He was even able to overcome the injustice, a bitter circumstance considering they were innocent. Verse 25 says at midnight Paul and Silas were praying and singing hymns to God. What was his mind set on? Anger? I get mad thinking about these men arrested illegally and beaten without a trial. Did you know the Romans had a very advanced system of law? Philippi, the city where this occurred, was a Roman province. (Read Acts 16:36–40 to see Paul's response when released. That's when he got angry.)

When I consider how it was for them in those circumstances and place myself there in stocks with back bloodied, my last thought would be to sing. Pray, yes, as in "God help me," but I don't see myself singing. I do see a lesson: singing praises to God as they did was a sign of robust joy. Where did Paul get it?

He considered it a privilege to suffer for the cause of Christ. We all know suffering happens in this world when good people confront evil. When they proclaim truth against deception and stand against injustice, suffering is on the way. Paul knew Jesus suffered though innocent. And he knew Jesus's teachings about rejoicing when in despair.

Several years ago, I went through a four-week counseling course to treat PTSD, depression, and anxiety. The sum of all I learned may be stated as "perception is king." Changing my view about the surrounding issues helped me manage the more troubling aspects of each one. I still work on the way I look at things to guard my mind and try to remember how perception determines reactions. Remembering enables me to change other areas of my life that could destroy relationships. This principle applies to choosing joy.

A simple rule to follow is this formula:

Event + Response = Outcome.

It's that simple and that hard to practice. When a mindset of joy is experienced, it's easier to cultivate from that perspective and grow the habit of choosing your responses.

If you keep your mind focused on things you enjoy, you save yourself from dwelling on problems and threatening issues. This balances your perspective to the positive side of the equation. Positives in life frequently outweigh the negatives. Even when they don't, there's no benefit attained by focusing on the negative issues. Acknowledge them? Sure. But don't swim in them.

Another way to cultivate joy is by giving it to others. Of course, it is tough to do when feelings are low, but giving comfort to others helps take our mind off ourselves. Giving joy supplies a purpose for living, but be sensitive if you encounter a person in desperate circumstances. Ask yourself first how best to provide them joy? What would I do if asked how to have joy when their life is filled with the effects of sexual abuse? What if I encounter someone held in slavery of some sort, would I tell them to find joy in spite of being enslaved while I stand there free? (Slavery is practiced, even today, in almost all, if not every country.)

If you try giving comfort in hopeless circumstances, clichés won't cut it. It would be better not to try than give out some trite quote or verse of Scripture and walk away. I don't have a pat answer for alleviating such suffering. But if I encounter someone trapped in impossible circumstances, then love requires me to do what I can. Feelings of helplessness will urge me to ignore deep needs. However, duty as a Christian calls my name. At those times I go to prayer and ask God to help me to find a way to give joy to someone hurting. One way, maybe the best way, is just sitting and listening.

Before doing something like this, see if the following warning fits your circumstances. If you're overwhelmed and barely able to function throughout the day, don't go looking for trouble by taking on more than you can handle. Leave it to others to step in for now and allow them to give joy to others in dire need of help. When our emotional or mental state is weak, we must be sure we don't get pulled down into that deep dark hole of someone else's troubles.

Otherwise, being on a forum where others are going through similar struggles may be okay. I occasionally peruse a PTSD site and offer words of encouragement when I can. It gives me joy knowing others understand some of what I'm going through. Even then, I cannot stay on that site for long because exposure to so much pain depletes me.

Having joy is a euphoric feeling when pain and sorrow are absent. Regardless, one has a choice to make room for it even in distresses. I read somewhere that the natural state of us all is joy. This thought encourages me to seek that natural state—the one taken away by violence.

If I keep a perspective of thankfulness, it goes a long way to making room for joy to happen. When blissful joy comes, even as a flash, try to nurture it. Turn your focus to the smallest positive things in life. Do you not have something positive? Here's something—the effort you're making to find healing in your life is very positive and powerful. All because you haven't given up. Give joy a chance to grow and it gains a firm place in our state of mind.

The last thing to leave you with before going on to study peace is this question:

When was the last time you allowed yourself to spend time dwelling on the wonders of Heaven? Dwelling on the love, joy, peace, and safety of Heaven goes a long way toward developing joyfulness. Eternity in Heaven vs. this short time of suffering on earth led Paul to write in 1 Corinthians 4:17, "For our light affliction, which is but for a moment, is working for us a far more exceeding and eternal weight of glory."

Affliction is defined as pressure, literally or figuratively, anguish, burdened, persecuted, in tribulation, trouble.

Points to Consider

☞ Joy is a frame of mind, and you can choose a joyous mindset.
☞ Joy can be developed by focusing on sound, positive truths. These verses are a worthy starting place: Colossians 3:1–2. They go back to thoughts of Heaven where Christ is.

I use the verse in 2 Corinthians 4:17 to keep my perspective in balance when I begin to focus on this troublesome but temporary world. It reminds me to reset my gaze heavenward to where God waits to give a crown for the pain endured here. This truth also offers a measure of peace.

LOVE

JOY

PEACE

MOVING IN THE SPIRIT—FRUIT OF THE SPIRIT

CHAPTER 15

Peace

"Peace I leave with you, My peace I give to you; not as the world gives do I give to you. Let not your heart be troubled, neither let it be afraid." John 14:27

IN THE EARLY EIGHTIES DURING THE fall of the year, I backpacked with a buddy and his wife in the Joyce Kilmer-Slick Rock Wilderness. This is in North Carolina. We broke camp on the early morning of our last day on top of a mountain called Hang Over. We were in the wilderness several days, and I was reluctant to leave, so I loitered behind. My friends left camp, headed down the trail leading to our vehicle far below in the valley.

I hoisted my pack, shuffled along the narrow ridge, and stopped at an overlook before the trail began its steep descent. The laurel there was only knee-high. I could see across the Tennessee River Valley where Lake Fontana lay and to the Smokies in the bluish smoky distance.

As I stood there, something happened that I never experienced before. A deep sense of peace overcame me. I felt it as a definite presence. I couldn't move, glued to the spot, and all I could do was let this wonderful feeling flood me. I breathed in the cool mountain air and looked around at the 360° view.

Was the view causing this peace? I didn't know. Far below, I could hear my friends' faint voices; the wife was asking where I was. Her husband said I would be along when I got ready. I smiled, knowing I needed to go, but still couldn't tear myself away. The feeling was one of divine peace and I didn't want to lose it. I did leave moments later and have never again experienced anything close to it.

What I felt was a sample of how it must be in Heaven. Why God allowed me to experience this at a time when I wasn't even living for Him remains a mystery. To this day, nearly 40 years later, I can close my eyes to revisit that moment and still feel a measure of that deep sensation of peace. Recalling that time and other lesser times of peace encourages me to keep looking for it most days, but like joy, we must have room for peacefulness to come in.

With this in mind there are two aspects of peace to consider: The first aspect is to receive peace; be open to it. Create circumstances conducive to peace. The second is to give or make peace. The latter resembles the peace that comes when two warring nations sign a peace treaty.

In my law enforcement career, the legal definition of my job duties was "peace officer." My sworn duty was first and foremost to keep the peace. How a peace officer goes about doing this makes for a long list.

For a Christian, it may help to know something of the nature of peace. How do you describe it? What is your idea of peace, either being at peace or peacefulness? Your perspective plays a big part in acquiring peace, but it is not the only factor. It's hard to be at peace in a warzone, but not impossible. It is this characteristic of divine peace that I want to focus on most of all—having peace when all hell is breaking loose.

Pondering where peace originates brings a ship's anchor to mind. Sailors facing a tempest make for a sheltered harbor. As soon as they arrive, they set out anchors to hold the boat steady in the hurricane. Anchors in place enable sailors to find peace in the storm. Even though tossed about, their faith in the anchor gives peace.

Does a Christian have an anchor, and if so, where is it placed? Look at Hebrews 6:18 and 19. In the last part of verse 18 "... who have fled for refuge to lay hold of the hope set before us." The Christian lays hold of hope as an anchor. Verse 19 describes anchor placement: "This hope we have as an anchor of the soul, both sure and steadfast, and which enters the Presence behind the veil..."

Jesus's atonement placed the anchor of Christian hope within God. The reference "behind the veil" is symbolic. It refers to God's presence in the Holy of Holies within the temple.

Your faith comes to play here through the choice to have hope-filled peace. It requires belief and trust that your soul is safe within God. Colossians 3:3 assures the Christian "died," symbolized by baptism, and now your new spiritual life is hidden with Christ in God. Read this with care. Let it soak in a little: your soul is safe within God. Allow peace to soothe your troubled soul.

Hope is the anchor. It's hard to see this when things feel hopeless, but stay with me here. We're going to see that regaining lost hope begins with focusing thoughts above, not on things of the earth. Colossians 3:2 (paraphrased). This is the principle mentioned earlier about renewing the mind.

Now, look at the last part of Hebrews 13:5 in which God promised, "I will never leave you nor forsake you." Promises in Scripture belong to every one of us, and all because God said to Abraham He would bless his Seed, singular. This is a reference to Jesus. Since Christians make up the body of Christ, God's promise to one member of the body is a promise to the whole body. This includes you, beloved of the Lord.

Spurgeon wrote about this truth in his Morning and Evening devotional. You find it in the February 23 morning reading. Here's an excerpt of that devotional:

"No promise is of private interpretation. Whatever God has said to any one saint, He has said to all. When He opens a well for one, it is that all may drink. When He opens a granary door to give out food, there may be a starving man who is the occasion of its opening, but all hungry saints may come and feed too. Whether He gave the word to Abraham or Moses, matters not, O Believer; He gave His promises to you as one of the covenant seed."

Here's where you make a choice whether to believe God's promises are for every Christian, or not. I write this to all who choose to believe. If you believe this, return to the last part of Hebrews 13:5, and reread the promise. What does this have to do with peace? Everything.

Believing that God will "never leave nor forsake you" is something to inspire hope. But not with the attitude "well, I'm hoping it's all true." Rather, having the conviction that our hope rests in God's inability to lie. And because He will never lie, I know He is with me, always. I can have this hope regardless of how it all feels at any given moment. So, hope is the anchor securely moored in the Son of God's love for each one of us. Dwell on this truth long enough and it allows a sense of peace to bless you. This is the peace Jesus said He gives us (John 14:27), but it comes with a condition. Jesus said we are not to let our hearts be troubled, which is another way of saying "don't dwell on troubles."

Instead, take a few moments to dwell on this: Scripture promises peace for all who believe in the finished work Christ did on the cross. In Ephesians 2:14–15, Paul writes, "For He Himself is our peace, who has made both one, and has broken down the middle wall of separation, having abolished in His flesh the enmity, that is, the law of commandments contained in ordinances, so as to create in Himself one new man from the two, thus making peace." Paul is describing how Jesus reconciled us to God. The middle wall of separation was sin. He removed the barrier between the human race and God, a similar theme to that of Colossians 1:19–22.

God's work, the action He took to reclaim His creation, makes it possible to have peace with Him. I enjoy knowing that when I face God and give an account of my life, it will be for reward, not condemnation. In Romans 8:1–6, Paul wrote an explanation of how to be at peace with God. He included an instructive measure that, if implemented, ensures God's peace. If you have time, read through Romans Chapter 8 yet again. It's worth the time.

Romans 8 is the Gospel encapsulated. In it, Paul explains the reasons peace with God is possible for all who choose it. Now, this is spiritual peace on a spiritual level. We must separate spiritual peace from peace found in favorable circumstances. Both are desirable, but spiritual peace is safe within God. This is how we have peace with God and the peace of God. You cannot have the second without having the first.

There is a Biblical example of how important it is to think right about things. (Especially concerning oneself in light of the new identity given to every Christian.) It's in Colossians 2:4–15, which goes into several facts about thinking rightly. Have you ever perceived effects different from what they were intended to convey? I read an example once about this tendency. It concerns dry ice.

Dry ice seems to give off smoke and if you touch it barehanded, it feels like fire burning the skin. Now, I did this once, picked up a piece of dry ice from a cooler in the grocery store. I only lifted it a few inches with my bare hand and it felt like holding a live coal. I dropped it fast. Upon observing this, my wife burst out laughing so hard it was embarrassing. Then she pointed to a sign on the cooler written in red lettering: "Warning—do not touch the ice without gloves." I saw that sign before opening the cooler; I really did. I just didn't think it would be that cold.

The point is though dry ice looks like it is smoking hot and feels like it's burning with heat when touched, the opposite is true. The appearance of dry ice does not convey the truth about dry ice. May I ask something here, how is life going for you right now? Are circumstances stacked against you? Is your back against the wall? Those realities scream defeat in your ear. I've heard them before; I know feelings agree with apparent truth. Conditions can look hopeless and may be so for the moment. But wait—put your troubled mind on hold for the moment.

Go back and read the first two chapters of Colossians and read once more Chapter 8 of Romans. These chapters and others throughout the Bible contain your birthright. Your destiny is written right there in God's Word. It's set in stone, safe in Heaven. Also, in John 14:2, Jesus offered this truth: He already went ahead of us and made ready a place for us to dwell.[49] Spurgeon tells us that promises like this one are equivalent to a check made out to each of us. All we have to do is take them to God as the heavenly banker and cash them in by faith, then draw out peace.

Peace comes to those who seek it and those who make allowances for it even in small measures. Again, you do this by dwelling on select passages of Scripture. It may challenge you to do this right now. I've mentioned this before and it bears repeating here. What is more difficult? Staying stuck in your circumstances or doing what is necessary to make a change? At least, if we turn our mind's focus away from adverse circumstances to positive things, it makes for peace. We help ourselves move along the process of feeling better.

At some point down the road, your efforts bring about peace. Efforts like ones described in this chapter bring results, no matter how slight. Peace in even small amounts is better than the alternative. This principle works only when implemented consistently.

A final issue of peace is how God uses it, or the lack thereof, to guide us in making decisions. For example, when desiring to change jobs or housing, go to God in prayer, and ask what to do or how to proceed. Ask God for peace about the correct decision. Pay close attention because this is where many Christians lose their way.

A formula may be helpful: When seeking God's will in any matter, first check to see if what you intend to do is forbidden in the Bible. If it is, don't do it, period. If it's not prohibited, then it's okay to seek Godly counsel from other Christians who are mature in the faith.

Next, will the decision hurt anyone? If so, don't do it. This step requires discernment when it involves something like a move to another state or country. What is an opportunity for one spouse may be seen by the other spouse as harmful, especially when children are affected.

And then, are you capable? I may want to be president, but I'm not capable.

What is your heart's desire? If you're not living in willful sin, then you have the freedom to choose. When making a decision, God's peace is sometimes evident from the very beginning or may come only after much agonizing prayer and loss of sleep. It happens both ways.

Truth to Consider

You are never without God's presence close to you,
wherever you go, whatever you do, no matter what
you're going through, regardless of how you feel at
any given moment. Bring this truth to mind often.
It brings peace.

Patience is necessary when waiting for peace. Especially when
needing a ceasefire for our soul to find rest. It's no coincidence the
next chapter is...wait for it...

LOVE JOY PEACE **PATIENCE**

MOVING IN THE SPIRIT—FRUIT OF THE SPIRIT

CHAPTER 16

Patience

"Strengthened with all might, according to His glorious power, for all patience and long-suffering with joy."
Colossians 1:11

"Knowing that the testing of your faith produces patience."
James 1:3

THIS CHAPTER WAS A TOUGH ONE to write. Most of what I want to portray in this chapter is the virtue that I lack: to be a patient man.

There are two aspects of patience to study: feeling patient and acting patient. The first state, feeling patient, may be hard to experience. The second is normally the daily struggle, that of acting patient regardless of feelings to the contrary. Being patient is an exceptional virtue to practice and one that kept me out of jail on a couple of occasions. Being patient kept my anger in check when I encountered aggressive drivers.

The patience required when dealing with people like aggressive drivers is one of two types described in the Bible: forbearance or endurance. It takes endurance to be patient when around irritating and annoying people. Also, without patience, I'm sure to damage the claim I represent the Son of God.

During Jesus's life on earth He exercised the patience of both forbearance and endurance. He had to. His disciples required both. He had to bear with them when they were slow to understand and when they were unkind to people coming to Him for help.

When they fumbled at social graces, patience led Him to kindness.Other times He was patiently stern if necessary. Like the times they were stubborn. And He needed endurance when they failed to support Him. You know, the way they abandoned Him and left Him to die on the cross pretty much alone. And then (and this is wonderful), His great forbearance while hanging on the cross when the priests mocked Him. It took supreme endurance to survive six hours hanging there while keeping His wits about Him.

How important is it to exercise patience as forbearance? The highest example I know of is Jesus on the cross. Priests mocked the one holding power over the angel armies. Jesus, by one act of patient endurance, spared all life on earth from annihilation by an angelic force. When I imagine the scene in Heaven, I can see angels leaning forward, hands on their swords, waiting for a signal from the Son of God. A summons that never came. Jesus died instead. He died for you. He died for me.

On the human level of patience, the kind with which I struggle, patience is a matter of perspective. Patience is hard work when instinct or habit calls for action, especially, action contrary to the teachings of Scripture. To help understand the importance of reacting with patience, think of it as a reaction based on kindness. Usually, my impatient responses aren't kind.

My perspectives about patience are a filter that determines whether I react with kindness or rage. When I went through counseling, years ago, I learned that anger is a choice, that I choose to be angry. Hearing that fired me up. I asked what else could I do when confronted with a threat against myself or another—just sit by and say, "Oh well"? My counselor was very patient. He kindly smiled and explained that anger isn't necessarily wrong; Jesus at times became angry. It's what I did with anger and how I reacted from that point forward that determined which actions were right or wrong. To control my temper meant learning how to increase levels of patience. This control is necessary.

If you struggle with a need for patience, pray for God's help with it; confess your desire for it; ask Him to make you patient. Have you ever heard someone say, "Never pray for patience?" My grandmother, Maw-Maw, used to warn me not to ask God for patience. She said it in such a way that I believed something terrible would happen. What? I never knew. Regardless, when the time came, I did ask God for it.

The issue came to the fore when I was teaching a men's class at church several years ago and the topic of patience came up. I told how Maw-Maw had warned me. One of the men asked why I would fear asking God for something He desires us to have. I looked at him in silence. Didn't everyone know the answer? He was surely testing me, but he sat quietly, waiting for an answer. Those who teach know what it's like being put on the spot. I didn't have a ready answer for him though I did wish he'd stayed home.

Still, it got me thinking. Why should I be afraid to ask God to teach me patience? What was the worst thing that could happen? I didn't want to overthink it, so I jumped in. You know how it is when you're afraid of something odious or fearful, and then you come up against it, palms sweaty and stomach tight, and something pushes you to face it? Just do it, as the commercial says. I'm like that with certain things. Take heights, for example.

First of all, I'm not afraid of heights, per se. I like rock climbing, rappelling, sky diving, and hang gliding. But still, when standing at the edge of a cliff and fear brings on that gut reaction of self-preservation, I get the urge to jump. That's right, jump. It's even better if there's water below. It must have something to do with wanting to overcome fear by doing exactly what makes me afraid.

I had the chance to test this theory once. Before leaving a friend's place on a Sunday afternoon, he said to check out a diving platform by the pond on the way out his driveway. As I drove by, I saw a small wooden platform high up in a tree (I found out later it was 40 feet off the water).

I stopped the car.

A strange urge to jump off that platform came over me. I walked to the base of the tree upon which boards nailed cross-ways formed a makeshift ladder leading up to the platform. I started climbing. When I reached the platform and stood looking down at the water, it happened. The realization I had to jump. My wife at the time stood below with the children, and I hollered down to her that I was going to jump. She asked what about the church clothes I had on. They were the only nice clothes I owned at the time. I thought yes, that's a good excuse not to jump while wearing dress clothes.

But no, that wouldn't work; I had to jump and was going to do so no matter what it took. I walked to the edge and looked down. Forty feet may not sound very high, but when I gazed down at the water, it felt high. I tried to jump but couldn't. Too afraid. I counted to three. Didn't work. After several more tries, I got frustrated. I couldn't do it, not on my own. So I started leaning forward until I leaned too far to catch myself, and that's when I fell. It wasn't pretty, either. I gave a virile yell, but I may have cried all the way down; I'm not sure. Then, I smacked the water while still leaning forward and my arms wind-milling out to the sides. I had hit the water hard, and it hurt. The force of the water peeled my eyelids open. I went all the way to the bottom so hard my boots stuck in the mud. Deep enough that I had to reach down and pull them free before swimming to the surface about eight feet up.

When I crawled onto the bank, I looked up at the platform and started climbing again. My wife asked what I was doing. Going to do it again, I told her. Why? She wanted to know. Because I didn't jump just now; I fell. I have to jump. I had to prove to myself I had enough courage to make the jump. I got to the top this time and didn't hesitate. Afterward, riding home soggy wet, water oozed from my Dingo boots. Smugness comforted me against the sneaky feeling I was an idiot.

So, where were we? ...asking for patience. I did ask God for it after the class when I had been asked why I was afraid. God didn't wait long to begin the lesson. The following weekend I spent a couple of days as a driving instructor for police recruits. The training facility was about eighty miles from home. I took the opportunity to ride my BMW motorcycle there. When I left at the end of training,

I took back roads, headed to an appointment later in the day. Since I don't like being late, I left early to cover minor contingencies.

I ran headlong into a lesson about patience. God had it waiting for me at a railroad crossing. In all the years I traveled this route, beginning in high school fifty years ago, I never saw a train cross there. It was a spur line; obviously, no trains used it very much. Waist-high weeds grew between the tracks to verify this.

On that day, not only was a train coming, but it was slow and long. It brought me to a standstill only because a very cautious driver blocked my way. She had stopped before the arms ever started down. So I stopped too, ...in disbelief. Because we both could have made it across the tracks. Then, I remembered having asked for patience. Oh, I see. It's a lesson. I cut the engine, put the bike on its stand, and sat back to wait. As I thought about what was happening, a satisfying feeling came over me, a sense of peace. Isn't that odd? I thought patience resulted in frustration and anger, not calmness, but there it was.

Recently, while wondering if I should use this experience as an example for this book, I asked my wife. I told her about that day at the tracks and the peace I had experienced. She asked, "So what happened?" I scowled, "What do you mean?" She gave me a patient look, "Why didn't the lesson take? Because you are not a patient man." A shroud fell away from my mind, and, at that moment, I realized the toll of my having been impatient with her throughout the years.

I may as well confess everything while I'm at it: I recently discovered that my impatience is rooted in pride. It took deep soul-searching to see this, to recognize conceit was the root. I should add that it's an attitude of prideful-superiority. This is astounding to consider because any goodness I have or any good I may have done for others has originated from God as a result of His mercy and His patient love. To see myself as morally superior to any person is despicable. It's one more testimony to the deceitfulness of sin.

Action to Consider

On a 3x5 card, write "Patience is being kind = peace"
That's it. Carry it with you and practice this for
several months as necessary. God will see to it that
patience becomes a habit. It will get easier as time
goes by. Repetition is the key. Repetition is the key.
Be patient.

Postscript—This is your chance to be patient with me. I have to
tell you what happened recently during a weekend getaway to the
mountains with my wife. First, I prayed for God's help, and then
I told her what I intended to do: I would practice being patient. I
asked if she minded me driving. You see, she would rather drive
to curb my irritation with other drivers, but what better way to
train? She agreed, reluctantly. Sensing her doubts, I resolved not
to disappoint her. We set out. As I drove along, I caught myself
muttering under my breath about a couple of drivers. Then it hit
me, I was feeding the impatience, and it, in turn, fed frustration. So
I stopped thinking ill of other drivers and instead pictured them
in a positive light. Maybe they were having a tough time like me.
The result was awesome. We had an enjoyable weekend driving
through the mountains and spending time together. The absence
of my griping and complaining about other drivers allowed Kris
to relax and so did I.

CHAPTER 17

Kindness

"Therefore, as the elect of God, holy and beloved, put on tender mercies, kindness, humility, meekness, and long-suffering;" Colossians 3:12

WHAT IS THE KINDEST THING ANYONE ever did for you? Remember how it felt? Kindness is something done for another person. Love may be a feeling at its best, but kindness is love in action.

Kindness is usually easier to practice than patience, but the rewards are immediate and satisfying. You can practice kindness right now. Want to try it? Next time you eat out tell the server how much you appreciate their hard work, and watch them smile. Also, consider going to the kitchen and thanking the cook for a good meal. The smiles are worth the effort, and it takes only a couple of minutes.

The definition of Biblical kindness is being merciful or having pity. It's being gracious, showing fondness and love toward others. It's gentle, having fraternal affection and love for other Christians.

Jesus is the best example, all the while living in challenging times and often surrounded by tough circumstances. Now, Jesus had a serious side of Him, balanced by kindness. Jesus was all about following the teachings of Scripture. In doing so, He confronted the religious hypocrites of His day. Even then, these confrontations were acts of kindness. He meant the clashes for their benefit. He was trying to bring them to repentance and spare them eternal damnation. The hostilities between Jesus and the religious crowd were also acts of kindness to the common folk, the ones suffering from ruthless priests-pretenders.

In this setting of religious oppression, compassion moved Jesus. Many times He encountered people hurting from unholy oppression. There is little wonder He drew large crowds. Jesus's compassion was kindness in action. Living among the people and not above them gave Him plenty of opportunities for kindheartedness.

You see, for the most part, Jesus hung out with the poor and lower class of society. But once, a prominent man named Simon invited Jesus to dinner at his home. The odd thing about this? Simon was a Pharisee.[50] These are the guys who would later incite the Romans to arrest Jesus and execute Him. Regardless, Jesus accepts the invitation and goes in. While He sat by the table, likely low to the floor and without chairs, something happened. An event unfolded that would embarrass most men. A woman, whose reputation was that of a great sinner, came to Jesus and knelt by his feet. She began to weep. Her tears fell onto His feet so she took her hair and started wiping them, washing them with her tears. Then she kissed Jesus's feet. She took a flask of fragrant oil and anointed them.

Can you picture this scene? The silence was surely complete, with everyone wondering what Jesus would do about the breach of social protocol. It was a violation of Jewish law for a woman to even touch a rabbi. Let me ask what you would do in Jesus's place? There you are at dinner, the guest of honor, when an unknown woman comes up to you crying and kneels before you. Her tears drop onto your bare feet, and she touches you. To make matters worse, she wipes the tears off your feet with her hair.

Using her hair as she did was an exceptional and intimate act. It's the kind of thing most husbands and wives never do for each other, much less for a stranger. The Pharisee, Simon, is offended and immediately condemns Jesus though he did it silently. He reasoned within himself if Jesus were indeed a prophet, He would have known this about the woman.[51] It's fair to assume Simon sat there smug with his deduction. Which raises the question: why did he invite Jesus in the first place since the majority of Pharisees hated Him? What else but to show his guests Jesus was nothing more than a vagabond. Now he saw for himself Jesus had no regard for social etiquette to begin with and no respect for religious law. How dare Jesus call his fellow Pharisees hypocrites?

So the room was silent except for the soft weeping of the woman. Instead of first reacting to the woman, Jesus responded to Simon. He told Simon He had something to say, and then told a story of two men who owed money to a creditor. One owed a large amount and the other small. When neither could repay the debt the creditor freely forgave them both (a constrasting practice in those days was sending the debtor to prison). Jesus asked Simon which of the two men would love the creditor more. Simon guessed the one who owed more. Jesus said he judged rightly.

Jesus then rebuked Simon for ignoring a fundamental act of hospitality. Simon didn't give water for Him to wash His feet and neglected to greet Jesus in the customary manner of respect.

Jesus next turned the indictment from the woman to Simon, and He completed her restoration by telling her, "Your sins are forgiven." This statement offended some at the table. They began asking among themselves, "Who is this who even forgives sins?" but Jesus said to the woman, "Your faith has saved you. Go in peace."

In light of this, how can we practice kindness today? I mentioned earlier how easy it is to express gratitude to a server in a restaurant. Every day we have opportunities to be kind in a similar fashion. There are hurting, lonely people everywhere. A visit to any nursing-home confirms this. Those irritating people in traffic could very well be going through some dire circumstances. Enough to bring tears to the most cynical Christian man I know: D Franklin Bradley. They need kindness instead of the irritation they may provoke.

Another easy way to show kindness is with words. The following are a few examples:

☞ Words of affirmation. Telling someone you believe in them.

☞ Words of sympathy. Just saying you're sorry for their loss.

☞ Words of love. Affection spoken is priceless when we tell someone how much they mean to us. Or write it in a note if easier.

[Speaking of writing, take time to write a letter or send an email to those who are important in your life. Share why they mean so much to you and, if applicable, let them know how much you appreciate all they have done for you over the years. This will send their spirits soaring. Years ago, a coworker told me how her father, who lived in another state, was filled with regret. His regret stemmed from the time he had lost with her due to his busy work schedule when she was a child. She said he was a good father and she understood why he worked so much back then in order to provide for his family. I asked if she had ever told him. She hadn't. Why not write it out in a letter to him? Her mom called her the night the letter arrived. When her dad began reading the letter, he suddenly got up, went downstairs, and wept. He called later and said it meant so much to know he wasn't a failure as a dad.]

☞ Words of forgiveness. Put the words in writing if they are too painful or uncomfortable to say in person. It doesn't mean a relationship has to develop afterward. That depends on the totality of the circumstances, whether it's possible or even desired.

Truth to Consider

Any deliberate effort at kindness brings results. From a smile to tears of joy, it is worth the effort given. To develop habitual kindness, go back to the 3x5 card technique again. Use the question 'Am I being kind?' Sometimes it's nothing more than holding your peace when a server is having a bad day. We cannot always know what another person is going through. The worst thing to be guilty of is adding grief, stress, and despair to someone already on the ropes.

One last thought comes to mind before closing this chapter. God revealed kind-hearted thoughts for you in Hebrews 13:5b: "For He Himself has said, 'I will never leave you nor forsake you.'"
Kindness is a good thing. Studying it is a great way to prepare for the next chapter, goodness.

CHAPTER 18

Goodness

"Now I myself am confident concerning you, my brethren, that you also are full of goodness, filled with all knowledge, able also to admonish one another." Romans 15:14

THE DEFINITION OF BIBLICAL GOODNESS IS virtue and beneficence. As a virtue, goodness ensures we follow God's law. (Although there's no need at this point to belabor the necessity of obeying God's commands.)

As a virtue, goodness ensures we do right by others. Virtue includes acts of integrity when faced with the urge to hedge and waffle on truth.

Doing good unto others as beneficence is an act of giving a benefit to others. For example, being charitable is beneficence. Goodness as benevolence is a vital component of love.

Paul is a prime example of goodness at work and how it can change someone's life. He was a Pharisee before becoming a Christian. Yes, he was a member of the same group responsible for Jesus's crucifixion. Paul described himself in Philippians 3:5 as a Pharisee; he then contrasted that with 1 Corinthians 15:9. Here he called himself the "least of the Apostles" because he persecuted the people of God. In Acts 26:9–11 Paul described in more detail his duties while serving the Sanhedrin, the ruling religious council in Israel at the time. They issued the death warrants Paul carried.

Paul recounts his story in Acts 26:9–11.

During Paul's time on the warpath, he was called Saul. He was an enraged man, a religious bigot of the most dangerous kind, and he had a governing body empowering him to kill Christians. He believed he was doing a good deed by hunting down Jews who believed their Messiah had come.

Paul changed when Jesus met him on the road to Damascus. The encounter changed him from a man of murder to a man of goodness. The unholy monster formerly dedicated to killing Christians became one of them. In time, he became a leader in the rapidly growing Christian movement. He even went so far as to include despised Gentiles in his outreach. Paul became a sterling example of goodness at work. What is this power that can change a killer, and what makes it available to us?

Let's examine the event on the road to Damascus that changed Paul to see if it contains the answer. Acts Chapter 9 verses 1–31 describes Paul was on his way to Damascus from Jerusalem. He carried letters of arrest for any man or woman he found who were of the Way. The Way was the name of followers of Jesus before Christian came into use. As he neared Damascus, a light from Heaven shone around him; Paul later described the light as brighter than the sun.[52] That must have been an extremely powerful light because Paul says it prompted him to fall to the ground. When He was on his face, a voice came from Heaven and asked: "Saul, Saul, why are you persecuting Me?"

Acts 26:9–11

"Ideed, I myself thought I must do many things contrary to the name of Jesus of Nazareth. This I also did in Jerusalem, and many of the saints I shut up in prison, having received authority from the chief priests' and when they were put to death, I cast my vote against them. And I punished them often in every synagogue and compelled them to blaspheme, and being exceedingly enraged against them, I persecuted them even to foreign cities."

Paul replied, "Who are you, Lord?"

"I am Jesus, whom you are persecuting. It is hard for you to kick against the goads." (According to Easton's Bible Dictionary, a goad is "an instrument used by ploughmen for guiding their oxen....

The goad is a formidable weapon. It is sometimes ten feet long, and has a sharp point.")

Paul, trembling and astonished, asked, "Lord, what do You want me to do?"

Do you see the submission of Paul, and how his obedience released the power of God? Will the power of God bring goodness in your life and mine? Submitting to God is the hardest thing to do, and I'm not talking about half measures. Full submission of your will is required here, even though it's also a lifelong process. God's call for submission allows only two possible responses: run from submission (think Jonah), or submit and ask God like Paul did when he said to Jesus, "Lord, what do You want me to do?"

If you read all the letters of Paul in one sitting, a few themes emerge. One of these is the moral excellence of Paul. He urged his readers to use his life as a guide, as he urged in 1 Corinthians 11:1, "Imitate me, just as I also imitate Christ."[53]

Paul's life is definitely worth imitating. Though, he could be stubborn, as some men describe it; he held strong convictions. Paul was humble, loyal, and faithful to his calling. His life was the personification of goodness in every aspect of meaning. After Jesus met him on that dusty road to Damascus, he never wavered throughout the rest of his life. He went on from there and lived in steadfast obedience to God's desire to save sinners.[54]

In the last days of his life, Paul wrote to Timothy, his "son" in the faith. "I have fought the good fight; I have finished the race; I have kept the faith." In short, Paul was a good man. He kept the faith until his death, not long after writing those words, when he died at the hands of Roman Emperor Nero.

Does viewing Paul's life as a guide to goodness mean I have to be perfect? If the Bible contained accounts of only perfect people who lived perfect lives, where is my comfort in any of it? Instead, God inspired the writing of Holy Writ, and He ensured the whole truth about His people came out. You know about King David don't you? Doesn't it help knowing God used people like Paul and King David? Despite their failures, God used them by bringing good from their bad. Our Lord promises the same for each of us.[55]

What benefits do you enjoy from having goodness around you? Do you live in a country where there's relative safety due to law and order? It is the result of moral virtue written into law and is a form of goodness.

Doing what is always right is goodness seen as integrity. Where would our world be today if men and women did not practice integrity in everything they did? It offsets some of the wrong done every day, the kind seen on the news. How much more peace would we have if those holding positions of leadership always did what is right?

An important fact about goodness to keep in mind is this: if you equivocate over issues requiring firm integrity or vacillate over issues requiring complete honesty, you will compromise your testimony as a Christian every time. There's no middle ground here. Any Christian who doesn't stand firm on issues requiring God-like character will side with evil. Friendship with the world is enmity with God.[56] Friendship with the world means acting and reacting according to the world's ways of doing things. It happens with Christian-based schools and organizations, even churches. When an embarrassing event occurs, leaders decide to minimize the effects and hide it, deny it, and, at times, in the process, fail to protect innocent victims from outright criminal behavior of their staff, or by their students.

Why am I hitting so hard on this? For the victims' sake. Also, if victims are not defended by leaders responsible for protecting them against evil, it persecutes Jesus, Himself.

Why did Jesus go after the frauds of His day in religious leadership positions? He did it because of the offenses against God and for the victims. Those in positions of leadership in Christian organizations bear the name of Christ. It's worth taking note that Jesus didn't go after the Romans; He spared them for the time being. He did not spare those who misrepresented God, for they abandoned their God-given authority. Instead, they gave glory to Satan by erroneous, smug interpretations of God's Word. They ignored its rule for them to reveal goodness. Jesus condemned this kind of leadership for the evil it perpetrated, all in the absence of the goodness they professed.

Enough said about that; time to end on a positive note.

Actions to Consider

☞ Always be truthful with someone, tempered with kindness.

☞ Be useful to someone in need.

☞ Visit shut-ins who are lonely.

☞ Be a big brother or sister to a child.

☞ Volunteer at shelters for the homeless and hungry.

☞ Run errands for someone without a car or unable to drive.

☞ Take an elderly grandparent to lunch or the park.

Are you overwhelmed but still want to do good for others, yet don't have the mental or emotional strength to do so? Then, pray for others in need. Praying is an important way to help others find goodness in their lives, even if they never know you prayed for them, you know, and so will God.

Having a spirit of goodness requires faithfulness to the principles covered in this chapter, those of integrity and honesty. Faithfulness is a comforting attribute of God. Faithfulness for the Christian is part mindset and part action.

CHAPTER 19

Faithfulness

"**Most men will proclaim each his own goodness, But who can find a faithful man?**" Proverbs 20:6

FAITHFULNESS IS SIMPLY FAITH IN ACTION, portrayed as loyalty and trustworthiness; faithfulness as a Fruit of the Spirit is a verb.

When Solomon was king of Israel, faithful people were rare. I take Solomon's statement in Proverbs 20:6 to mean people who were faithful in all things were uncommon. Around us, we see faithful people, but only to a degree.

How is your sense of faithfulness? Have you examined it recently, or better yet, has it been tested lately? It seems only by testing is the depth of our faithfulness revealed. Being faithful is imperative to God; He will test the depth of it. How does He go about this? In the old days of sailing, when a ship neared shore, sailors tested the water's depth under the hull by lowering a weighted rope with knots tied at regular intervals. When the rope bottomed out, they counted the knots and knew whether to change course to avoid shipwreck.

When God tests a person's faithful capacity, He measures how we respond to circumstances. He alone knows how to accurately measure the depth of faithfulness in every soul exposed to adverse events in life. Our Lord measures faithfulness to show us the measure of our integrity and not for His knowledge; He already knows we are made of dust.[57] Before looking at Biblical faithfulness further, what follows are examples of faithfulness seen at times on national news coverage.

Faithfulness is that admirable trait revealed when someone intervenes selflessly during a high-profile event, say, a school shooting spree or shooting in a workplace or mall. In several instances of faithfulness, unarmed bystanders confronted shooters, and a few lost their lives in the process.

In combat, faithfulness is displayed in so many ways. Sometimes, it is falling on a grenade, and other times, it's going out on patrol day after frustrating day. It's standing firm in a firefight and protecting your buddies' flanks.

For many of us, it's the quality of getting out of bed every morning to look after our children. Single parents have it especially tough. They have no one to fall back on, such as when they must respond to a child's needs, regardless of being sick, themselves.

It's the motivation to go to work and face the same drudgery, week after mind-numbing week. Faithfulness brings the spouse home after work. It protects the marriage from infidelity by steering a man or woman home when the job is stressful, instead of frequenting places where temptations to stray are rife.

Faithfulness shows up in class when the temptation to cheat rears its ugly head and whispers, "Go ahead, do it. Everyone else is."

Spiritually, it's a type of faithfulness to obtain eternal life, evidenced by belief and trust in the manner God requires from every soul, that of believing unto salvation. It returns faithfulness to God. The Apostle John wrote in 1 John 1:9 concerning God's faithfulness, 'If we confess our sins, He is faithful and just to forgive us our sins and to cleanse us from all unrighteousness.' God is faithful; He is committed to fulfill His promises in His time. He is trustworthy to do all He has promised.

God's faithfulness to creation is such that if He so desired and retracted His command for creation's existence, everything—the earth, the galaxy, the universe—would disappear. There wouldn't be a grain of dust left, nothing and no one to accuse God of not keeping

His promises. He does not need to change. Besides, a perfect being has nothing needing improvement. Therefore, Almighty God is perfect in His faithfulness to us. He will never rescind His sustaining power for creation's existence or the existence of His love for each one of us.

God is faithful to the characteristics of love, mercy, kindness, etc. Believing this truth brings comfort of the best kind.

At the far other end of the spectrum of faithfulness is that of a dog. I once read that examples of faithfulness of a dog are used more often than examples of faithfulness of a person. I don't know if that's true, but a dog's loyalty is sometimes legendary. In the 1920s or 30s in Japan, a dog named Hachi had a master who died soon after Hachi came to live with him. For the next decade, every day, this dog went to the train station in the morning where his master used to board the train, bound for work. There, Hachi waited, all day, every day, returning home each evening. He did this act of faithfulness until he died.

Faithfulness in Galatians 5:22 expresses the idea of standing fast—to stand firm for what is right, regardless of the consequences. The same idea appears in Ephesians 6:11 and 13. Paul used the analogy of wearing armor to stand against the wiles of the devil, and to withstand the evil day, that is, to remain faithful during an onslaught. Finally, in Ephesians 6:18, he encouraged his readers to pray and be watchful with perseverance.

The fact that perseverance is needful reveals difficult times will happen at times when I must take a stand and be faithful to do what is right. There are definite benefits to developing faithfulness as the Holy Spirit imparts it. We are, first of all, children of God through faith: Galatians 3:26; we are blessed: Proverbs 28:20; we will have eternal life with God: 2 Timothy 2:11; God is going to reward all who live in faithful obedience to His teachings: Matthew 25:23.

The benefits of faithfulness are several, and though you might suffer for being faithful, don't draw back in fear or dread. The blessings that come to you in eternity will offset the costs. It takes faith to believe, despite any feelings of weakness to the contrary.

God knows I'm dust in the scales when compared to Him, but He takes it into account when placing His nature of faithfulness in me. In Revelation 2:10, Jesus insisted that Christians remain faithful, even to death, for He will reward them—and us—with the crown of life. That counsel goes for every follower of Christ.

I want to end this chapter with an appeal of my own. For great examples of faithfulness, please read the last words of several well-known Christians, asssembled at the website listed in the Endnotes.[58] The following chapter is about gentleness. Jesus was gentle with all who came to Him in sincere need. And though He could be fierce with His enemies, He was always gentle with the hurting and sick among the crowds. He is the perfect example of gentleness.

CHAPTER 20

Gentleness

"I, therefore, the prisoner of the Lord, beseech you to walk worthy of the calling with which you were called, with all lowliness and gentleness, with long-suffering, bearing with one another in love," said Paul in Ephesians 4:1, 2

PAUL WROTE TO THE EPHESIAN CHURCH while imprisoned in Rome. His letter to the Ephesians contains several themes. Among them, conduct befitting a Christian. It's interesting that Paul listed gentleness as one of the virtues to remember.

Gentleness is the opposite of harshness. Consider Matthew 11:25–29, "At that time Jesus answered and said, "I thank You, Father, Lord of heaven and earth, that You have hidden these things from the wise and prudent and have revealed them to babes. Even so, Father, for so it seemed good in Your sight. All things have been delivered to Me by My Father, and no one knows the Son except the Father. Nor does anyone know the Father except the Son, and the one to whom the Son wills to reveal Him. Come to Me, all you who labor and are heavy laden, and I will give you rest. Take My yoke upon you and learn from Me, for I am gentle and lowly in heart, and you will find rest for your souls.'"

Jesus offered an invitation for His listeners to join Him. He then described His gentle and humble heart. He said the effect of joining Him is one of rest. In context, Jesus had recently rebuked two cities that had rejected His works. It seems Jesus was concerned that those listening might be a little skittish of Him, afraid to draw near.

After all, He had recently pronounced destruction on those two nearby cities. (He characterized them as worse than Sodom in their hardhearted opposition to repentance.)

Is it possible He softened His message by offering assurance He is gentle and humble in His heart? I know it can be hard coming to God on His terms. Before I understood God better, I was afraid I would never measure up, so why even try? It felt safer to keep my distance from God. That was before I learned how tenderhearted He is and how tender Jesus is even now.

In verse 29 of this passage in Matthew 11, Jesus urged his listeners to learn from Him. He wanted them to know how gentle He is with all who trust Him. He wants us to learn the same thing. He promises to give rest if we join Him in a relationship, but one grounded in tenderness; He called this "yoked together" with Him. The rest from toil He offered was from the impossible burdens placed by the religious crowd of that day. These were the ones who ruled in Jerusalem. How burdened are we by demands for performance? Too burdened to be gentle? Do you have that short fuse so common nowadays?

Gentleness, like the other virtues studied, is also best seen in action. There is always a choice when confronted by difficult, unwanted circumstances. Either react with harshness or gentleness. In John Chapter 8:1 – 12, the Jerusalem religious crowd confronted Jesus early one morning as He sat teaching in the temple. This was His custom when in town. The crowd approached, with Pharisees in control, determined to put Jesus in an impossible position. They dragged in a woman caught in adultery. They presented the case before Him and gave Him the opportunity to react to this violation of law. The law was clear in its harsh condemnation. Death, they said. Then they asked Jesus what he had to say on the matter. If Jesus were to say, "Stone the woman," they would triumph by manipulation and thereby strengthen their standing. If Jesus said, "Release her," they would triumph by impeaching His right to teach the law with authority, but Jesus outwitted them. He reacted with tenderness. On the surface, this may seem an easy choice: for Jesus to be gentle. But from the crowd's point of view, the circumstances surrounding the woman were dire, and Jesus held her life in His hands.

A little background about this particular morning: In this event, Jesus is the target of a conspiracy intended to trap Him into breaking the religious laws of Israel. If He broke the law by withholding His consent to kill the woman, it would provide a basis for His arrest. Those men seeking to have Him arrested were relentless. Instead of concern for the spiritual state of their nation, these self-righteous men focused on Jesus's death to the point of obsession. There was nothing they wouldn't do and no one they wouldn't sacrifice to destroy Jesus and His teachings.

After accusing her, they asked, "But what do You say?"

In response Jesus stooped down and wrote on the ground. He wrote in the dirt with His finger as though He did not hear the question. When they continued asking Him to answer, Jesus looked up and said:

"He who is without sin among you, let him cast the first stone." (paraphrased)

He again wrote on the ground.

Can you feel the tension? The woman's emotions are surely roiling in fear. How desperate did she feel in that moment of silence? She was trapped, snatched and thrust into the center of focused hatred. Her life hangs in the balance. Jesus's words will determine her fate, and, at this point, He hasn't argued for her. He isn't even looking at her or anyone else. There He kneels, writing in the dust. Curiosity caused those standing close enough to look at the words written there.

Regardless of what Jesus wrote, beginning with the oldest to the youngest, the mob drifted away. Only the woman remained. Now, what would you do if you had been standing there? Would you have lectured this woman? Pointed out how it was her fault for doing something so sinful? "Reap what you sow, you know."

Not Jesus. He stood and asked where the woman's accusers were. Had no one condemned her? "No one, Lord." "Neither do I condemn you; go and sin no more." In other words, go and leave her life of sin. Those were tender words coming from a rabbi who had every right under the religious law of that day to condemn the woman to death. Instead, He offered tender restoration so she could live in the light of His love. To go and sin no more would bring her out of the darkness of her despair.

Continuing with John 8:12, Jesus spoke once more to the people he had been teaching earlier. "I am the light of the world, He who follows Me shall not walk in darkness, but have the light of life."

The Pharisees in that crowd were the first to react to these words from Jesus. It's possible He spoke for the benefit of the woman likely still standing nearby. Can you blame her? It was far safer with Jesus than back home. Then Jesus continued to speak words of comfort by teaching how to leave a life of sin: follow Him. The implication being to follow His teachings and their result is a life of light.

There were others also gathered in the temple that morning who Jesus needed to learn tenderness. His disciples were there—the men later entrusted with the Gospel message. But before that happened, Jesus wanted them to learn gentleness.[59] Did the lesson take? It may have with time, but there were other times gentleness was nowhere to be seen in these men. On occasion, they shooed away children drawn to Jesus. At other times, they urged Him to rid them of people in desperate need who clamored to be heard.

Once, in a foreign city in the region of Tyre and Sidon, a Greek woman lived. She heard Jesus was in town and came crying for Him to heal her daughter of demonic possession.[60] What did the disciples do? For that matter, what did Jesus do? At first He ignored her. Shocking, isn't it? With their leader ignoring the woman's pleas, His followers came to Him, but not to implore His help for her. They beseeched Him instead to send the woman away because "She cries out after us." See the exasperation? They had grown tired of hearing this mother plead for her daughter.

Why didn't they ask Jesus to heal the little girl? Where is the gentleness? Scripture doesn't tell us. As it turned out, Jesus tested the woman's faith by His initial silence. This revealed, if not a lesson in gentleness, then faith in action. One thing is sure: those men missed an opportunity to be gentle like their teacher.

I, too, missed an opportunity for gentleness years ago. My daughter was sixteen and had crashed her car while racing. I arrived at the scene and took in the wreckage. I looked at her and said, "You just had to learn the hard way, didn't you?" She wilted.

I can hardly bear to think back on her pain in that moment. She needed gentleness from me, and I reacted with anger instead of being thankful she was uninjured. All because she totaled her car. I have long since apologized to her and let her know how much I deeply regret what I did. Harsh words are like firing a bullet, you can't call them back. I learned a lesson that day about the need for gentleness. And I have used opportunities ever since to share that same lesson with other parents in similar circumstances, those involving a teenager who wrecked their car.

Here is one such occasion. Years after my daughter's accident, I was helping another officer direct traffic at the scene of an accident. A car pulled up. I looked over and saw that the father of the teenage girl at fault had arrived. He zeroed in on his daughter with a face of rage that said it all. I intercepted him and his wife, and took them aside to explain how I had handled my daughter in this same set of circumstances. I explained that his daughter had simply committed an error in judgment when she made a left turn into the path of an oncoming car, adding that there was nothing he could say right now that would fix that vehicle. I reinforced my counsel to be kind by pointing out his daughter could very well be dead, and that, with time, the shock of the moment would wear off, and all that would remain is what he said and did in the next few minutes.

He nodded in agreement, and I left him and his wife a moment alone. Afterward, they went to their daughter and hugged her as she apologized and cried. The father gave me a knowing look and a slight smile as he left the scene.

In James 3:17, gentleness is a benefit of wisdom, and it is grouped with purity, peace, mercy, and good works. Gentleness is when you forgo always having to be right. Yielding like this diffuses tense situations. It gives comfort to those wounded by self-condemnation. And it helps prevent lifelong regret from harsh words or actions.

Without God having to chasten you with regret for being harsh, is there a better way to develop gentleness as a habit? Is it possible to practice that habit daily? There is. But to do so it's helpful to view gentleness as related to two other virtues: kindness and patience.

When trying to become aware of habitual behavior, it's tough to recognize things like harshness. Especially small acts of it. To discover if you have a trait of harshness, ask someone close to you. But first a word of warning: it's difficult being told your faults and shortcomings. If you're already dealing with low self-esteem, be sure to ask someone who cares about you enough to tell it gently.

Another word of warning: If you're asked for an honest opinion about someone else's harsh tendencies, like whether they're impatient or unkind, your response may backfire on you. A friend once asked for an opinion concerning a habit he had about which he had been confronted at work. I agreed tactfully how it was true, yes, he had a temper, a problem with anger always just below the surface. I went on to say I recognized his anger because I, too, had a temper, though it didn't make me a bad person and neither did it him. He took it as a personal attack and, yes, got mad. He felt betrayed, that I was siding with this person at his workplace. Talking further with him accomplished nothing, and this experience ended our friendship.

However, if you have someone you trust, ask if they will help you pinpoint areas that require your attention. Focus on the "softer" virtues in Scripture—those such as gentleness, kindness, love, patience and forgiveness. Reflecting on the definitions of gentleness as meekness, mildness, and humbleness provides a broader context in which to view them. It also broadens the areas of practice.

A practical way to apply gentleness is by remaining calm no matter how bad the news you receive. In counseling, I learned to take a deep breath and a one-second pause before responding. Also, be kind in response to whatever and whoever comes against you, whether from good people or bad. I found the workplace rife with injustice dispensed by leaders who didn't always respond with virtuous acts; instead, they responded with the opposites of those acts, with wickedness. I normally respond to injustice with harsh, bitter, and vengeful speech. You may imagine the outcome. It dinged my career.

You can facilitate the development of a calm, gentle reaction by writing on a 3 x 5 card how you intend to react in given circumstances. I have a 3 x 5 card on my console that reads, "When other drivers are aggressive, rude, and careless—pray for them." Using the 3x5 card reminder fortifies a mindset of gentleness and displaces inappropriate habitual responses such as anger.

To sum up this chapter, let's review a few benefits of being gentle in order to reinforce the message.

Truths to Consider

- ☞ Being gentle builds loyalty from both peers and subordinates in the workplace.
- ☞ It enables people to *want* to help you rather than hurt you as a way of retaliating against harsh treatment.
- ☞ Gentleness creates a sense of peacefulness in the home, rather than fear. Fear causes others to walk around on eggshells, a miserable way to live.
- ☞ Spiritually, it speaks well of the One we profess to follow because it points to a gentle Savior.

It takes self-control to become gentle, especially when we must bestow that gentleness upon those for whom we have no affinity.

LOVE JOY PEACE PATIENCE KINDNESS GOODNESS FAITHFULNESS GENTLENESS SELF-CONTROL

MOVING IN THE SPIRIT—FRUIT OF THE SPIRIT

CHAPTER 21

Self-Control

"But also for this very reason, giving all diligence, add to your faith virtue, to virtue knowledge, to knowledge self-control, to self-control perseverance, to perseverance godliness, to godliness brotherly kindness, and to brotherly kindness love. For if these things are yours and abound, you will be neither barren nor unfruitful in the knowledge of our Lord Jesus Christ." 2 Peter 1:5–8

WOULD IT SURPRISE ANYONE TO LEARN that most people in prison actually know right from wrong? Many times the reason someone lands in jail is a lack of self-control. I worked in a jail for two years and sometimes talked with inmates about their lives. They shared their stories about how their own poor choices had landed them in jail. Many people besides the criminal element also find themselves caught up in trouble from a lack of self-control. At times, I've had to ask myself why I did what I knew was wrong while turning a blind eye to the consequences? I found the answer surprising.

Simply put, I had carelessly chosen which teachings from the Bible to obey and which ones to ignore. The ones I ignored I did so by diminishing them in my mind, demoting them to less importance in the great scheme of things. This was dangerous thinking. And self-control was one of those.

In old English, the definition for self-control is temperance. The term is taken from a word meaning masterful, in the sense of mastering an appetite. Its opposite is having no limits, being without restraint. This describes a life out of balance.

An extreme result on the positive side of self-control was the Puritan lifestyle. Theirs was an almost punishing restraint from anything pleasing or considered sinful. An extreme result on the negative side is self-hatred for failing to measure up to God's standards. Never mind God's promise in Romans 8:1, "There is no condemnation to those in Christ." Self-condemned people punish themselves in a number of ways. This includes cutting, which is a harmful means of relieving emotional pain. Do you see how both extremes are unnecessary?

Being one who prides himself as having strict self-discipline, I found my self-discipline not so strict in every area of my life. The professional attitude I carried as a police officer did not carry over into relationships outside work, and certainly not heavenward. For years I lived the Christian life as a double-minded man. I would think, "Let me have a little of that teaching, but don't include the discipline that requires me to forsake the lust of porn." I gave offerings at church only because it was called for. And I rarely gave out of love and never cheerfully. Money was an idol, and I lacked the self-control to confront the fact I was deceived by the lustfuness and riches of society.

A lack of self-control in my relationships revealed I did not seriously take the warnings and prohibitions in Scripture about sin, such as adultery. They are in the mind and heart first, you know.[61] The fact of the matter is that the mind is the battleground of spiritual matters, and here, self-control must take a stand.

Are you having difficulty controlling thoughts because of mental conditions as a result of trauma? It may take professional counseling to enable you to control your thoughts. Again, if you seek counseling take care to make sure the counselor is someone you trust. Check their references. During the first few sessions, go slow until a basis for trust has been established. Choose someone trained specifically in trauma, if available.

Regaining control of your thoughts is an important step to developing the other eight fruits (virtues). I have wondered why

Paul wrote self-control last when he listed desired traits. Logically, I would have placed it first. The reason being that self-control is necessary to enjoy the other virtues. I suppose Paul set down the others first to create a desire in the heart for the remaining virtues. With desire in place, he provided the way to acquire all of them: by the exercise of self-control.

Since this is the last chapter, I want to look at the most important act of self-control recorded in the Bible. The following story is how God restrained Himself using self-control. What makes this tragedy unique is that the people in question had assaulted the very Son of God in their lack of control.

Please allow me to retell what happened to Jesus on the day of His death. We'll look at Jesus's arrest, trial, and crucifixion with a focus on His self-control and how it saved the human race.

The night Jesus was arrested, numerous prophecies were fulfilled, specifically prophecies of His death. He had tried to prepare His followers earlier in the week when He told them He would be put to death at the hands of the religious authorities in Jerusalem. Peter rebuked Jesus for saying such things. Jesus countered by commanding Peter, "Get behind me, Satan." Jesus was telling Peter to get out of the way. Jesus's self-control did not allow Him to be swayed by Peter even though Peter had good intentions.

During the Last Supper, Jesus controlled events. He allowed Judas to leave the group so he could report Jesus's whereabouts (Jesus actually told Judas to go). Later, in the garden of Gethsemane, soldiers arrived with Judas in the lead. Jesus had to restrain Peter who wielded a sword in his attempt to protect Jesus. The great restraint of the Son of God began in earnest when mere men grabbed Him and took Him away for trial by the priests.

While Jesus stood before the priests, the beatings and mocking began. Jesus said very little throughout this ordeal, but one thing stands out. When asked by those interrogating Him whether He was the Son of God, Jesus answered, "You rightly say that I am." Jesus cannot lie, and so declared His deity to the men present. (That declaration still echoes forth today.)

The priests then turned Jesus over to the Roman governor Pontius Pilate. They made false accusations to incite the governor against Him. They insisted he put Jesus to death. Pilate questioned Jesus and found no fault in Him. But, to gratify the priests, he had Jesus severely flogged. During the flogging, Roman soldiers mocked Jesus as they beat Him without mercy. I wonder at the self-control of the angelic army of Heaven. They watched as their King was whipped bloody by a Roman instrument of torture.

The Romans used a multi-corded whip called a flagellum. It had sharp pieces of bone or rock sewn into each of the cords down the length and at the end. It was a fearful means of punishment often tearing the skin away from the back and exposing the rib cage.

This beating evoked no mercy from the priests, and, eventually, Pilate yielded to the demands he execute Jesus.

The soldiers mocked Jesus by placing a twisted crown of thorns onto His head. They bowed before him, saying, "Hail, King of the Jews!" If ever the fate of the human race hung in the balance, this was such a time.

Later, on the cross, Jesus displayed several acts of restraint. This is vital to understanding the benefit of developing self-control. Jesus exercised His self-control while having complete freedom to choose another option. He had the angelic army option. But, in the greatest act of love ever bestowed upon the human race, Jesus chose to submit to death. He did not change His mind in the midst of pain and humiliation. (Even as He hung by spikes driven through His hands and feet, with His back lacerated, and thorns stabbing into His head.) Jesus's self-control costs Him much more than the physical pain. His submission to His Father's will (His plan of redemption) incurred every bit of God's wrath. Wrath stored up from sin's effects throughout all time—all past, present and future sins.

Jesus's self-control unto death ensured the wrath of God against sin is now satisfied. This is why Paul could write in Romans 8:1, "There is therefore now no condemnation for those who are in Christ Jesus, who do not walk according to the flesh, but according to the Spirit." A Christian is saved not by works, but by grace.[62] This is stated emphatically in Ephesians 2:8. Self-control and restraint from sin are necessary for my relationship with God to work, to remain healthy and good. It's the same as between a parent and child, isn't it? The parent will always love the child, though at times, not all the child's behavior. If I want my relationship to God as Father to remain close, I must learn to trust Him and obey His teachings. My self-control is at work best when I choose to obey God instead of following my natural tendencies.

Keep in mind the focus of this book is restoration and freedom. Restoration comes from implementing the teachings put forth in this book, teachings taken from the Bible. Self-control begins in the mind. Freedom begins with a commitment to put in place the means of changing your mindset. Let self-control free you to live in the power of truth.

CHAPTER 22

Summary

"Abide in Me," Jesus, in John 15:4a. Abide in the Son of God for restoration from despair's devastation in the soul.

A NOTE TO CHRISTIANS:
Jehoshua Messiah, the Anointed One. Jesus is the Son of God. He loves you deeply and has a plan for your life. Although suffering is part-and-parcel of life on this earth, Jesus walked the road of suffering before us. Therefore, walk courageously from this day forward. Live as royalty of Heaven; God is not only your King, but also Father in the deepest sense. He promised to never leave you or forsake you. His Word written in the Bible must be trusted and used as a guide in all matters of life. Do this and use Biblical principles cited in this book to build upon the foundational promises of Jesus. Rise above the torment.

For any reader who isn't convinced, I understand. Being logic-minded, it took a long time for me to finally trust what I could not see, much less understand. The Son of God understands this reluctance to trust Him. It's the reason He performed amazing feats while on earth, such as walking on the sea during a storm. He also used other methods downright hilarious when teaching His followers to trust Him. He once had Peter go fishing and look in the mouth of the first fish he caught. Peter went fishing. He caught one. He opened its mouth and there he found a coin. That coin was the exact amount to pay the temple tax being demanded.[63] Jesus did such things to penetrate people's disbelief.

As humorous as it must have been, the outcome with the coin contained a message (as did the outcome when Jesus walked on the sea). The message? Supernatural power was at work in a Man born of a woman, but conceived by a Being from another dimension. Heaven isn't some place out there to the right of some star; on the contrary, it's near. The spiritual realm in which God dwells is close. But we can't see or perceive it with the senses we have. No more than we see ultraviolet light or hear sounds pitched too high. Please consider this if not a Christian: God waits for you to make a choice. If your choice is to reject claims of His reality, He remains patient and kind and still loves you. His Son died for you, regardless. If you choose not to believe Jesus died for your sins, remember something, please. To die without claiming God's forgiveness is to face God on your own, by your own merits. And be assured, He demands a perfect life.

You have the freedom to choose. I pray from the heart that you choose carefully.

To review, first, there are three points to cover, then, I'll summarize and close.

1. In the blueprint of building a life-bridge structure, Jesus gave five foundational promises. These were given at the beginning of His ministry. He offered hope in the forgiveness of sin, all sins, by His death, burial, and resurrection from the dead. The promises covered in Step One, Part One, found in Luke 4:18 still stand firm today.

2. For Christians, there is power available for bridging over despair by obeying His commands in Step Two. Implementing the power of God by obeying His commands ensures change will occur in any life. This occurs by applying Biblical principles. And this means take action. Actions which displace destructive beliefs

and habits causing much despair. Displacement is an ongoing process. You have to do the work, there is no other way. I wish it were easier.

3. Any life lived in the power of obedience is evidenced by certain traits or virtues called Fruit of the Spirit. Those who strive as best they can to live in the ways of the Spirit will see these virtues develop in their life. They are like markers on the road of life, giving a sense of direction. This fruit must be cultivated, enjoyed along the way, and given to others. Remember, perfection is not required. When the Bible talks of Christian perfection, it means, for the most part, maturity. However, when God looks at you, Christian, He sees perfection in His Son. He attributes it to you because His Son Jesus gave His perfect life in exchange for yours. This is the new birth necessary for life in Heaven.

My prayer is for you to become one with Him in spirit; one in thought and actions. At its core, one with Jesus means to become a servant to all. I discovered this only recently. In keeping with this discovery, I opened my life in this book to all who may learn from my mistakes. Take as personal possession every bit of encouragement possible. See in the Bible what God did and is doing for you, His precious child.

I want to thank each one of you for joining me in this study. If the message within these pages helped, please share the lessons learned.

May God, the Father, and His Son Jesus, by the power of the Holy Spirit, bless you and keep you.

Notes from the Author

On Salvation

The sum of salvation is the restoration of the lost relationship with God.

Salvation is not church membership, good works, being sprinkled with water, or any other manmade, man-imposed ritual.

Spurgeon writes this about salvation: "This is the royal road to comfort. Great thoughts of your sin alone will drive you to despair; but great thoughts of Christ will pilot you into the haven of peace." [64]

[A note to Christians: The details of Salvation are provided here for the benefit of anyone reading this who is not a Christian. Please bear with any repetitions]

What is salvation, the Biblical need to be saved, in its essence? First of all, salvation is a legal procedure required by God before any may enter Heaven.

How does someone complete the legal procedure?

Picture this scene: A man or woman is standing before God, guilty of sin against God. This sin is treason against the rule of God and carries the penalty of death. The Son of God steps forward and declares the guilty one innocent of all crimes against the realm. Innocent, that is, if the guilty looks to Jesus to take away their sin. The Bible declares Jesus took upon Himself every guilty person's sin and discharged the penalty. (We have only to ask forgiveness based on this exchange.) This legal act satisfied the requirement of God's law, that a perfect life is forfeited to pay the penalty of sin.

How is this possible? The legal term Biblically speaking is atonement. Jesus atoned (paid) for all sins by His death on the cross.

Because He atoned for sin, forgiveness is available to all who ask for it. Salvation is free.

Why is salvation necessary to begin with? Because the first man and woman, Adam and Eve, sinned by disobeying God in a matter for which the penalty was death. Their act infected the human race with the very sentence of death God so sternly warned them about. This may seem harsh, but I ask you to consider something written in the Bible on page one of Genesis. It says, "In the beginning God created..." Therefore, God has the right to rule over all He created, as well as a right to impose a just penalty for rebellion against His rule.

Beyond this declaration, we must believe salvation is necessary. God declares Himself throughout the Bible as a holy Being. This means He isn't like any of the human race in essence. He did create our race in His likeness by instilling our ability to think, understand and comprehend why, and experience emotion. But compared to us, He is Supreme in every aspect of the word. He is the giver and sustainer of life.

According to the Bible, God has every right to set forth a rule of law for His creation. This includes every human being. With the laws of conduct He set forth, He also reserves the right to impose penalties for violations of His law. Every violation of God's law is a personal affront to Him and His holiness.

When a person acts contrary to law, they assume responsibility for the consequences. This goes for government law and God's law. Concerning God's law, every person must decide whether to believe God is absolute ruler over all we know. And as such has the right to judge the human race according to its conduct. Judgment may occur against nations or individuals. Final judgment will occur for every person who has ever lived and will happen after the end of this current age. The Bible describes this judgement in Revelation 20:11 as the "great white throne judgment." At this judgment, faith plays a crucial part in that with faith, it is possible to escape judgment at God's throne.

Why must anyone die for sin, especially the Son of God? It's actually the heredity of sin that's the culprit. Look around. There are many examples of sin and its effect on the human race. When is the last time you heard someone say, "Why on earth did they do that? It was so cruel." Or, "How could he kill a child?" Are reactions like this indicative of the fact that people know there is good and evil and that evil is wrong? Do we know instinctively evil should be punished?

This is why in God's order of things, He requires the death penalty of sin, for the act of rebellion, treason actually. Sin is evil. Period. Death as the penalty is not as far-fetched as it may seem at first. Though harsh, many countries today still have death for treason on the books. There are many who find this revolting. It's because they don't understand the depth of evil, but God does. It's why death is God's curse on our race because of sin. But it's too complicated to examine all the arguments about it. Others more learned have investigated this point and written extensively on the subject. To pursue deeper knowledge of this issue, you'll find several books on the topic listed in Resources.

With all sin punished and atoned for at the cross—past, present, and future sins—God offers all people a complete pardon from the death penalty. But, this pardon must be deliberately chosen, personally, by each person who wants God's offer. No one can do this for you. If you choose God's pardon and ask for it, in that instant, your name is written into the ledger of Heaven.[65] God forgives, but only when asked for forgiveness based on Jesus's death on the cross. So, how does this work out in reality, right now? Meaning how does someone ask?

On Prayers for Salvation

What follows are sample prayers that anyone may pray. The prayers are dedicated to complete forgiveness of sin and result in new spiritual life, both now and for eternity.[66] These prayers may be prayed silently or aloud, alone or with another. Praying to ask God for a new life is a sacred and holy act. It must be done in faith. How much faith? Jesus said faith the size of a mustard seed is sufficient.[67]

Sample Prayers

Examples of Salvation Prayers—Pray one of these or your own prayer if it's the same in essence.

First Sample Prayer for Salvation:

Lord Jesus, I know I am a sinner. Please forgive my sin by Your death on the cross. Come into my life and be my Savior. Help me live for You from this day forward. In Jesus name, Amen.

Second Sample Prayer:

God in Heaven, I come to you in the name of Jesus. I admit to You that I am a sinner, and I am sorry for my sins. I need Your forgiveness—please Forgive Me.

Third Sample Prayer:

God, I believe Your only Son Jesus Christ shed His blood on the cross and died for my sins, and I am now willing to turn from my sin.

I confess You Jesus as the Lord of my soul. With my heart God, I believe that You, God, raised Jesus from the dead. I commit myself to Jesus Christ as my personal Savior, and, according to His word, right now I am saved.

Thank You, Jesus, for your death on the cross that saved me. By Your Spirit, lead me into repentance. Lord Jesus, transform my life so that I may live for Your glory, that I will honor You with my new life. Amen.

For anyone who prayed one of these prayers or something like them in essence, welcome to the family! Becoming a Christian involves adoption into God's family as a child. That makes us brothers and sisters in the faith.

A word of exhortation: Do everything possible to find a church with sound Biblical teaching. At the very least, if you have the Internet, there are lessons and sermons online and church services archived. Numerous resources exist to help provide guidance to new Christians. I have listed a few ministries I trust and invite you to view these while asking God to provide the information He knows is right for you.[68]

Resources

Use the resources listed below for further study to help maintain spiritual balance. These resources may be found online and most Christian book stores carry these titles, as well. I use Christianbook.com.

- ☞ Look into Lee Stroble's book series *The Case for Christ* and *Case for Faith*. They are an excellent source of knowledge on Christian beliefs.
- ☞ *Morning and Evening* by Charles H. Spurgeon
- ☞ *My Utmost for His Highest* by Oswald Chambers
- ☞ *The Pursuit of God* by A. W. Tozer
- ☞ *The Pilgrim's Progress* by John Bunyon
- ☞ *The Practice of the Presence of God and Teachings of Brother Lawrence*
- ☞ For Bible study, Bible.org is a very good source and it's free.
- ☞ e-sword.net is free Bible software. An excellent resource for study and lesson or sermon creation. It's a free download and contains commentaries, different Bible versions, devotionals, and *Strong's Concordance*. If you send a $25 donation a CD is sent for download. It contains several more Bible versions than the online copy.
- ☞ myptsd.com—For any with PTSD this site helps even if all you do is read the threads. This site helps with feeling connected.

Glossary

NKJV   New King James Version of the Holy Bible

KJV   King James Version with some old English

PTSD   Post Traumatic Stress Disorder

TBI   Traumatic Brain Injury

Atonement   Appeasement of God's wrath against sin; payment for sin. On the cross Jesus's death atoned for all sin, for all time.

Salvation   The process which delivers a human being from Hell and places all who choose salvation into a restored relationship with God. It is being saved from the penalty of sin. This process involves a person being born again, born as a spiritual child with God as Father.

Sanctification   To be set apart, made holy in the Biblical sense. The Holy Spirit sanctifies the Christian through the truth of God's Word in the Bible. It's an ongoing process throughout the Christian's life on earth.

Redemption   The debt Jesus paid to set us free from condemnation. It was as if we were held prisoner, a hostage for ransom and Jesus paid that ransom with His life.

Justification   A legal term signifying acquittal. Christians are justified to stand before God, innocent.

Regeneration   New birth spiritually and, as such, means every Christian has a new beginning. The slate is wiped clean as far as God is concerned.

References

e-Sword® is a free Bible program made available by Rick Meyers. An electronic copy may be obtained at www.e-sword.net, or to obtain a CD, send a donation to e-sword.net/support.

Morning and Evening by Charles H. Spurgeon is a daily devotional taken from his best sermons. I have read this daily since March 2003. Spurgeon teaches covenant theology. This is the belief God enters into a covenant with Christians. It happens by God giving certain promises in the Bible. We can find peace since He's placed Himself in a covenant relationship with us. This devotional contains much encouragement for struggling Christians.

My Utmost for His Highest by Oswald Chambers. This is another daily devotional helpful in my walk with God. (Especially as it relates to understanding relationship issues between God and His people.) It is a compilation of Chamber's radio messages and sermons given to Bible college students and contains some pretty deep theology. It helps keep me on the path.

The Pursuit of God by A. W. Tozer is a great, practical book for those who hunger for God's presence. In this great read, I learned about how to cultivate friendship with God.

The Practice of the Presence of God by Brother Lawrence. This book is a collection of letters between Brother Lawrence, a monk, and a Cardinal. It reveals how easy it can be to develop a daily relationship with God.

About the Author

D. Franklin Bradley is a survivor. Having endured a tough child-hood, he then went on to lose his marriage of 30 years because of poor choices. David spent 21 years in law enforcement only to retire with PTSD. These hardships toughened him and enabled him to survive, to become a Hope-Warrior.

David is stubbornly on fire with this message of hope. He knows the danger of suicidal depression, from both sides of the gun. Now, he is a fighter in the sense of striving to get off the ropes when life puts him there. His life's mission is to share the survival skills he has learned.

He is also a spiritual seeker—a Christian who is not content with the mere trappings of religion but hungry for the presence of God. He feels it is his duty to put forth the truth about the value of the human soul—souls for whom he believes the Son of God died to save.

David says motorcycling is good for the soul and, for therapy, frequently rides to his favorite coffee shop in Athens, GA.

Endnotes

1   Spurgeon expounds on this verse – morning reading for 3/6.

2   Matthew 7:26, 27: "But everyone who hears these sayings of Mine, and does not do them, will be like a foolish man who built his house on the sand: and the rain descended, and the floods came, and the winds blew and beat on that house; and great was its fall."

3   1 John 4:8, 16: "He who does not love does not know God, for God is love." "And we have known and believe the love God has for us. God is love, and he who abides in love abides in God, and God in him."

4   Quote 1 Corinthians 1:9: "God is faithful, by whom you were called into the fellowship of His Son, Jesus Christ our Lord."

5   James 1: 2-4: "My brethren, count it all joy when you fall into various trials, knowing that the testing of your faith produces patience. But let patience have its perfect work, that you may be perfect and complete, lacking nothing."

6   Ephesians 1:18: "...the eyes of your understanding being enlightened; that you may know what is the hope of His calling, what are the riches of the glory of His inheritance in the saints,"

7   Ephesians 1:18

8   John 8:36: "Therefore if the Son makes you free, you shall be free indeed."

9   Luke 6:48, 49: "He is like a man building a house, who dug deep and laid the foundation on the rock. And when the flood arose, the stream beat vehemently against that house, and could not shake it, for it was founded on the rock. But he who heard and did nothing is like a man who built a house on the earth without a foundation, against which the stream

beat vehemently and immediately it fell. And the ruin of that house was great."

10   Ephesians 4:5 "one Lord, one faith, one baptism;"

11   *Foxe's Christian Martyrs of the World* by John Foxe, an eye-witness to several Christians being put to death for their faith.

12   John 17:15-18: "I do not pray that You should take them out of the world, but that You should keep them from the evil one. They are not of the world, just as I am not of the world. Sanctify them by Your truth. Your word is truth. As You have sent Me into the world, I also have sent them into the world."

13   Romans 6:4

14   Romans 6:4: "Therefore we were buried with Him through baptism into death, that just as Christ was raised from the dead by the glory of the Father, even so we also should walk in newness of life."

15   Matthew 3:13-17: "Then Jesus came to Galilee to John at the Jordan to be baptized by him. And John tried to prevent Him, saying, "I need to be baptized by you, and are You coming to me?" But Jesus answered and said to him, "Permit it to be so now, for thus it is fitting for us to fulfill all righteousness." Then he allowed Him. When He had been baptized, Jesus came up immediately from the water; and behold, the heavens were opened to Him, and He saw the Spirit of God descending like a dove and alighting upon Him. And suddenly a voice came from heaven, saying, "This is My beloved Son, in whom I am well pleased."

16   John 3:3, 16: "Jesus answered and said to him, "Most assuredly, I say to you, unless one is born again, he cannot see the kingdom of God." "For God so loved the world that He gave His only begotten Son, that whoever believes in Him should not perish but have everlasting life." In this passage

Jesus is explaining to Nicodemus the way to obtain eternal life. Nothing is mentioned at all concerning baptism.

17 Matthew 26:14-16: "Then one of the twelve, called Judas Iscariot, went to the chief priests and said, 'What are you willing to give me if I deliver Him to you?' And they counted out to him thirty pieces of silver. So from that time, he sought the opportunity to betray Him."

18 Revelation 5:6: "And I looked, and behold, in the midst of the throne and of the four living creatures, and in the midst of the elders, stood a Lamb as though it had been slain, having seven horns and seven eyes, which are the seven Spirits of God sent out into all the earth."

19 Luke 22:15: "Then He said to them, "With fervent desire I have desired to eat this Passover with you before I suffer;" John 13:13-17: "So when He had washed their feet, taken His garments, and sat down again, He said to them, "Do you know what I have done to you? You call Me Teacher and Lord, and you say well, for so I am. If I then your Lord and Teacher, have washed your feet, you also ought to wash one another's feet. For I have given you an example, that you should do as I have done to you. Most assuredly, I say to you, a servant is not greater than his master; nor is he who is sent greater than he who sent him. If you know these things, blessed are you if you do them."

20 Matthew 27:5: "Then he threw down the pieces of silver in the temple and departed, and went and hanged himself."

21 For more information concerning Jesus's last hours, read Chapters 13-17 in John.

22 Matthew 24 contains detailed prophecy of end time events.

23 1 Corinthians 3:11-15: "For no other foundation can anyone lay than that which is laid, which is Jesus Christ. Now if anyone builds on this foundation with gold, silver, precious

stones, wood, hay, straw, each one's work will become clear; for the Day will declare it, because it will be revealed by fire; and the fire will test each one's work, of what sort it is. If anyone's work, which he has built on it endures, he will receive a reward. If anyone's work is burned, he will suffer loss; but he himself will be saved, yet so as through fire."

24 Luke 18:34: "But they understood none of these things; this saying was hidden from them, and they did not know the things which were spoken."

25 Mark 16:14, 19: "Later He appeared to the eleven as they sat at the table; and He rebuked their unbelief and hardness of heart, because they did not believe those who had seen Him after He had risen." "So then, after the Lord had spoken to them, He was received up into heaven, and sat down at the right hand of God."

26 Acts 2:2

27 Jude 1:24

28 Romans 8:28

29 Ephesians 1:17 "that the God of our Lord Jesus Christ, the Father of glory, may give to you the spirit of wisdom and revelation in the knowledge of Him,"

Ephesians 1:18 "the eyes of your understanding being enlightened; that you may know what is the hope of His calling, what are the riches of the glory of His inheritance in the saints,"

30 Matthew 5:44: "But I say to you, love your enemies, bless those who curse you, do good to those who hate you, and pray for those who spitefully use you and persecute you,"

31 Luke 10:25-37 – This is a long passage and while too long to quote, one worth reading and meditating on the circumstances involved.

32   John 8:48: "Then the Jews answered and said to Him, "Do we not say rightly that You are a Samaritan and have a demon?""

33   Luke 23:34

34   Colossians 1:10b

35   I was taught while growing up in church and in some of the publications I used to read that if I lived a good life according to the Bible, then I would be blessed both spiritually and physically, with health and prosperity, and live a trouble-free life. These false teachings discount the numerous places where the Bible clearly teaches that in this life we will suffer as Christians, even when doing good. I believe this health-wealth teaching is rooted in pride for it says one who is prosperous and trouble free is approved of by God and therefore better than others, and those who suffer have hidden sin in their lives. Adherents to health-wealth and name-it-and-claim-it can be downright hateful to those of us suffering with ailments like depression. I know this from firsthand experience when I shared with a brother about going through depression. He lectured me about having sin.

36   Mark 12:41–44: "Now Jesus sat opposite the treasury and saw how the people put money into the treasury. And many who were rich put in much. Then one poor widow came and threw in two mites (maybe a penny), which make a quadrans. So He called His disciples to Himself and said to them, "Assuredly, I say to you that this poor widow has put in more than all those who have given to the treasury; for they all put in out of their abundance, but she out of her poverty put in all that she had, her whole livelihood." Parenthesis mine – Luke 21:1–4 records this same event.

37   Revelation 21:21: "And the street of the city was pure gold, like transparent glass."

38   Second Corinthians 9:7: "So let each one give as he purposes in his heart, not grudgingly or of necessity; for God loves a cheerful giver."

39 John 1: 4-5a: "In Him was life, and the life was the light of men. And the light shines in the darkness, and the darkness did not comprehend it."

40 John 10:10b: "I have come that they may have life, and that they may have it more abundantly."

41 Proverbs 13:24: "He who spares the rod hates his son, But he who loves him disciplines him promptly."

42 Read *Dare to Discipline*, by Dr. James Dobson.

43 A turtle on a fencepost had help getting there and we're all just like that.

44 Ephesians 5:26: "that he might sanctify and cleanse her with the washing of water by the word," In this passage Paul is describing how Jesus sets His bride, the church, apart for Himself and makes her fit, and by bride is meant the body of Christians as a whole.

45 Revelation 20:15: "And anyone not found written in the Book of Life was cast into the lake of fire."

46 1 John 4:16: "And we have known and believed the love that God has for us. God is love, and he who abides in love abides in God, and God in him."

47 Matthew 7:3

48 Luke 14:26: In this passage Jesus is warning that to follow Him fully requires all other loves be *hate* compared to love for Him. Only Almighty God has the right to require such devotion.

49 John 14:2–3: "In My Father's house are many mansions; if it were not so, I would have told you. I go to prepare a place for you. And if I go and prepare a place for you, I will come again and receive you to Myself; that where I am, there you may be also."

50 Luke 7:36–50. Grab your Bible. A reading of these verses is necessary to fully understand what Jesus accomplished here.

51 Luke 7:39: "Now when the Pharisee who had invited Him saw this, he spoke to himself, saying, 'This Man, if He were a prophet, would know who and what manner of woman this is who is touching Him, for she is a sinner.'"

52 Acts 26:13: "at midday, O King, along the road I saw a light from heaven, brighter than the sun, shining around me and those who journeyed with me." In this account Paul is being held for trial and is giving testimony to King Aggripa concerning the charges against him. For background into his arrest, read Acts Chapters 21 through 26.

53 1 Corinthians 4:16: "Therefore I urge you, imitate me." Also, for further study the following verses are helpful: Romans 8:37, 1 Corinthians 4:6, 14, 9:15, 10:6–11, 2 Corinthians 13:10, Galatians 5:17, 6:11, Titus 2:15, 3:8.

54 1 Corinthians 9:22: "to the weak, I became as weak, that I might win the weak. I have become all things to all men, that I might by all means save some."

55 Romans 8:28: "And we know that all things work together for good to those who love God, to those who are the called according to His purpose."

56 James 4:4–5: "Adulterers and adulteresses! Do you not know that friendship with the world is enmity with God? Whoever therefore wants to be a friend of the world makes himself an enemy of God. Or do you think that the Scripture says in vain, "The Spirit who dwells in us yearns jealously"?

57 Genesis 3:19; Psalm 103:14

58 christianity.co.nz/2016/02/life-after-death/#10

59 Second Timothy 2:24 "And a servant of the Lord must not quarrel but be gentle to all, able to teach, patient,"

60 Matthew 15:21-28

61 Matthew 5:27–28: "You have heard that it was said to those of old, "You shall not commit adultery." But I say to you that whoever looks at a woman to lust for her has already committed adultery with her in his heart."

62 Ephesians 2:8: "For by grace you have been saved through faith, and that not of yourselves; it is the gift of God, not works, lest anyone should boast."

63 Matthew 17:24: "When they had come to Capernaum, those who received the temple tax came to Peter and said, "Does your Teacher not pay the temple tax?"

Matthew 17:25: "He said, 'Yes.' And when he had come into the house, Jesus anticipated him, saying, 'What do you think, Simon? From whom do the kings of the earth take customs or taxes, from their sons or from strangers?'"

Matthew 17:26: "Peter said to Him, 'From strangers.' Jesus said to him, 'Then the sons are free.'"

Matthew 17:27: "Nevertheless, lest we offend them, go to the sea, cast in a hook, and take the fish that comes up first. And when you have opened its mouth, you will find a piece of money; take that and give it to them for Me and you."

64 Spurgeon's *Morning and Evening* – February 24th, Evening.

65 Revelation 21:27: "And there shall by no means enter it anything that defiles, or causes an abomination or a lie, but only those who are written in the Lamb's Book of Life." Revelation 20:15: "And anyone not found in the Book of Life was cast into the lake of fire."

66 John 3:15–16: "...that whoever believes in Him should not perish but have eternal life. For God so loved the world that He gave His only begotten Son, that whoever believes in Him should not perish but have everlasting life." John 10:28: "And I give them eternal life, and they shall never perish; neither shall anyone snatch them out of My hand."

67 Luke 17:6: "So the Lord said, "If you have faith as a mustard seed,..."

68 In Touch / Insights for Living / Focus on the Family / Love Worth Finding.